First World War
and Army of Occupation
War Diary
France, Belgium and Germany

56 DIVISION
Headquarters, Branches and Services
Commander Royal Engineers
5 February 1916 - 18 May 1919

WO95/2939/1

The Naval & Military Press Ltd
www.nmarchive.com
Published in association with The National Archives

Published by

The Naval & Military Press Ltd

Unit 10 Ridgewood Industrial Park,

Uckfield, East Sussex,

TN22 5QE England

Tel: +44 (0) 1825 749494

www.naval-military-press.com

www.nmarchive.com

This diary has been reprinted in facsimile from the original. Any imperfections are inevitably reproduced and the quality may fall short of modern type and cartographic standards.

© **Crown Copyright**
Images reproduced by permission of The National Archives, London, England, 2015.

Contents

Document type	Place/Title	Date From	Date To
Heading	WO95/2939-1		
Heading	56th Division C.R.E. Feb 1916-May 1919		
War Diary	Hallencourt	05/02/1916	26/02/1916
War Diary	Domart	27/02/1916	11/03/1916
War Diary	Doullens	12/03/1916	16/03/1916
War Diary	Le Cauroy	17/03/1916	05/05/1916
War Diary	Henu	05/05/1916	30/05/1916
Heading	56th Division. War Diary C.R.E. 56th Divisional Engineers. June 1916 Appendices 1 to 8.		
War Diary	Henu	01/06/1916	30/06/1916
Map	Key To Trench Map		
Map			
Miscellaneous	Cartridges for the purpose of destroying traverses and blocking enemy trenches. Appendix 1		
Map	Map Of The South 1/z Of Squares 3,4, & 5, Squares 9,10. & 11, & Part		
Map			
Map	France		
Miscellaneous	Appendix 2		
Miscellaneous	Appendix C.		
Map			
Miscellaneous	Appendix D.		
Map	Type Plan No 9. Sniperscope Scale 1/2 Inch 1 Foot		
Miscellaneous	O/C Party 1st London Regiment. Appendix 3	17/06/1916	17/06/1916
Miscellaneous	Appdx 3		
Miscellaneous	C.R/S 512. Appdx 4		
Miscellaneous			
Miscellaneous	Notes On The Use Of Bangalore Torpedoes Appdx 5		
Miscellaneous	Appdx 5		
Map	Type Plan No 10. Bangalore Torpedo		
Miscellaneous	C.R./S 614 Appdx 6		
Miscellaneous	Appdx 6		
Miscellaneous	Major Samuel Major Glover Appdx 7.	19/06/1916	19/06/1916
Miscellaneous	Appdx 7		
Miscellaneous	C.R/S No. 15. Appdx 8	26/06/1916	26/06/1916
Miscellaneous	Appdx 8		
Miscellaneous	Appendix A.		
Miscellaneous	Type Plan No 6A. Portable Bridge For Field Artillery. Scale 1/2 Inch To 1 Foot		
Heading			
Miscellaneous	Appendix B		
Map	Type Plan No4 Portable Bridge Scale 1/2 Inch-1 Foot		
Heading	56th Division. C.R.E. 56th Divisional Engineers. July 1916		
War Diary	Henu	01/07/1916	31/07/1916
Miscellaneous	C.R/S. 51.	07/07/1916	07/07/1916
Miscellaneous	C.R.E. 56th Division.	04/07/1916	04/07/1916
Miscellaneous	Headquarters, 56th Division	03/07/1916	03/07/1916
Miscellaneous	2/2nd London Field Co. 2.7.16	02/07/1916	02/07/1916

Type	Description	Start	End
Miscellaneous	2nd Lieut. H.A. Scott R.E. Officer i/c No. 1 Section 2/1st London Field Co.	03/07/1916	03/07/1916
Heading	56th Divisional Engineers C.R.E. 56th Division. August 1916		
War Diary	Henu	01/08/1916	20/08/1916
War Diary	Doullens	21/08/1916	21/08/1916
War Diary	Frohen	22/08/1916	22/08/1916
War Diary	St Riquier	23/08/1916	31/08/1916
Heading	56th Divisional Engineers C.R.E. 56th Division. September 1916. Appendices:- Notes on Training. Report on Work of R.E. & Pioneers.		
War Diary	St Riquier	01/09/1916	04/09/1916
War Diary	Corbie	05/09/1916	06/09/1916
War Diary	Forked Tree	07/09/1916	07/09/1916
War Diary	Billon Farm	08/09/1916	16/09/1916
War Diary	Battle H.Q.	17/09/1916	20/09/1916
War Diary	Billon Farm	21/09/1916	30/09/1916
Miscellaneous	Notes Of Training Of R.E. Company and Attached Appdx A	01/09/1916	01/09/1916
Map	Strong Point For A Platoon		
Miscellaneous	Report on Work of R.E. and Pioneers of the 56th Division in Somme Offensive Appdx B		
War Diary	Battle H.Q.	01/10/1916	09/10/1916
War Diary	Citadel	10/10/1916	10/10/1916
War Diary	Yzeux	11/10/1916	20/10/1916
War Diary	Hallen Court.	21/10/1916	24/10/1916
War Diary	Longpre	25/10/1916	25/10/1916
War Diary	Merville	25/10/1916	25/10/1916
War Diary	Lestrem	25/10/1916	27/10/1916
War Diary	La Gorgue	28/10/1916	31/10/1916
Miscellaneous	R.E. Operation Order No. 1.	25/10/1916	25/10/1916
Miscellaneous	Dispositions Of Brigade H.Q. and Battalions on Nights 26/27th to 29/30th October Issued With 56th Divisional Order No. 59.	24/10/1916	24/10/1916
Miscellaneous	Table "B".	25/10/1916	25/10/1916
War Diary	La Gorgue	01/11/1916	30/11/1916
Miscellaneous	56th Divisional Engineers Order No. CR/S 374. Appendix A	24/11/1916	24/11/1916
Miscellaneous	Revised Table of Reliefs. Appendix C	29/11/1916	29/11/1916
Miscellaneous	Continuation of 56th Divisional Engineers Order No. CR/S 374 Appendix B	29/11/1916	29/11/1916
War Diary	La Gorgue	02/12/1916	30/12/1916
Miscellaneous	56th. Divisional Engineers Order No. 75.	18/12/1916	18/12/1916
Miscellaneous	56th Divisional Engineers Order No. 76	29/12/1916	29/12/1916
Miscellaneous	In Continuation of 56th Divisional Engineers Order No.75.	22/12/1916	22/12/1916
War Diary	La Gorgue	01/01/1917	30/01/1917
Operation(al) Order(s)	56th Divisional Engineers Order No.77.	11/01/1917	11/01/1917
Operation(al) Order(s)	56th Divisional Engineers Order No.78	23/01/1917	23/01/1917
Operation(al) Order(s)	R.E. Operation Order No.79	31/01/1917	31/01/1917
War Diary	La Gorgue	23/02/1917	28/02/1917
War Diary	La Gorgue	03/02/1917	22/02/1917
Operation(al) Order(s)	R.E. Operation Order No.80. Warning Order.	23/02/1917	23/02/1917
Miscellaneous	56th Divnl. R.E. Order No.81.	24/02/1917	24/02/1917
Operation(al) Order(s)	56th Divisional Engineers Order No 82.	27/02/1917	27/02/1917
Miscellaneous			

Type	Description	Start	End
War Diary	La Gorgue	01/03/1917	06/03/1917
War Diary	Willeman	07/03/1917	07/03/1917
War Diary	Le Cauroy	08/03/1917	13/03/1917
War Diary	Gouyen Artois	14/03/1917	19/03/1917
War Diary	Beaumetz	20/03/1917	31/03/1917
Operation(al) Order(s)	56th Divisional Engineers Order No. 83.	13/03/1917	13/03/1917
Miscellaneous	Relief & March Table of 513th (London) Field Co. R.E.		
Operation(al) Order(s)	56th Divisional Engineers Order No. 84.	21/03/1917	21/03/1917
Miscellaneous	56th Divisional Engineers Order No. 85	22/03/1917	22/03/1917
Miscellaneous	56th Divisional Engineers Order No. 86	26/03/1917	26/03/1917
Miscellaneous	Amendment to 56th Divisional Engineers Order No. 86.	27/03/1917	27/03/1917
Operation(al) Order(s)	56th Divisional Engineers Order No. 87.	28/03/1917	28/03/1917
Miscellaneous	56th Divisional Engineers Order No. 88.	31/03/1917	31/03/1917
Miscellaneous	Work Report for Week ending noon March 21st 1917.		
Miscellaneous	Works Report for week ending noon 28/3/17.		
War Diary	Beaumetz	01/04/1917	12/04/1917
War Diary	Achicourt	13/04/1917	19/04/1917
War Diary	Covin	20/04/1917	25/04/1917
War Diary	Hauteville	26/04/1917	26/04/1917
War Diary	Warlus	27/04/1917	29/04/1917
War Diary	Arras	30/04/1917	30/04/1917
Operation(al) Order(s)	56th. Divisional Engineers' Order No. 89.	02/04/1917	02/04/1917
Miscellaneous	56th Divisional Engineers Order No. 90.	02/04/1917	02/04/1917
Miscellaneous			
Miscellaneous	Notes on Conference of O'S. C. 3/4/17.	04/04/1917	04/04/1917
Operation(al) Order(s)	56th Divisional Engineers Order No. 91.	03/04/1917	03/04/1917
Operation(al) Order(s)	56th Divisional Engineers Order No. 92.	04/04/1917	04/04/1917
Operation(al) Order(s)	56th Divisional Engineers Order No. 93.	07/04/1917	07/04/1917
Miscellaneous	56th Divisional Engineers Order No. 94.	18/04/1917	18/04/1917
Miscellaneous	Distribution of, and work done by, R.Es. and Pioneers during the operations S.E. of Arras, April 1917.	21/04/1917	21/04/1917
Operation(al) Order(s)	56th Divisional Engineers Order No. 95	27/04/1917	27/04/1917
Miscellaneous	56th Divisional Engineers Order No. 96.	28/04/1917	28/04/1917
Miscellaneous	56th Divisional Engineers Order No. 97.	30/04/1917	30/04/1917
Map	Details of Bridge Strutting		
Miscellaneous	C.R.E 56th Division.	04/05/1917	04/05/1917
War Diary	Arras	01/05/1917	21/05/1917
War Diary	Warlus	22/05/1917	24/05/1917
War Diary	Habarcq	25/05/1917	31/05/1917
Operation(al) Order(s)	56th Divisional Engineers Order No. 98	05/05/1917	05/05/1917
Miscellaneous	56th Divisional Engineers Order No. 99	10/05/1917	10/05/1917
Miscellaneous	56th Divisional Engineers (Warning) Order No. 100.	17/05/1917	17/05/1917
Miscellaneous	56th Divisional Engineers Order No. 101.	22/05/1917	22/05/1917
Miscellaneous	Issued With 56th Divisional Engineers Order No. 101. Appendix "A"		
Miscellaneous	56th. Divisional Engineers' Order No. 102.	31/05/1917	31/05/1917
War Diary	Habarcq	02/06/1917	11/06/1917
War Diary	Arras	11/06/1917	30/06/1917
Operation(al) Order(s)	56th Divisional Engineers Warning Order No. 103.	06/06/1917	06/06/1917
Miscellaneous	Relief Table to accompany Order No. 103.		
Miscellaneous	Amendment to 56th Divisional Engineers Order No. 103.	07/06/1917	07/06/1917
Miscellaneous	Headquarters, 56th Division.	18/06/1917	18/06/1917
Miscellaneous	Divisional R.E. Dump.		
Miscellaneous	The Two Advanced R.E. Dumps.		
Operation(al) Order(s)	56th Divisional Engineers Order No. 104.	27/06/1917	27/06/1917

Type	Description	Start	End
Operation(al) Order(s)	56th Divisional Engineers Order No. 105.	30/07/1917	30/07/1917
Miscellaneous	March Table To Accompany 56th Divisional Engineers Order No. 105.		
War Diary	Arras	02/07/1917	04/07/1917
War Diary	Sombrin	05/07/1917	24/07/1917
War Diary	Eperlecques	25/07/1917	31/07/1917
Operation(al) Order(s)	56th. Divisional Engineers' Order No. 106.	19/07/1917	19/07/1917
Miscellaneous	March Table Issued With 56th Divisional Engineers' Order No. 106.		
Operation(al) Order(s)	56th. Divisional Engineers' Order No. 107.	21/07/1917	21/07/1917
Miscellaneous	March Table Issued With 56th Divisional Engineers' Order No. 107.		
War Diary	Eperlecques.	01/08/1917	06/08/1917
War Diary	Reninghelst	07/08/1917	13/08/1917
War Diary	Dickebusch.	14/08/1917	18/08/1917
War Diary	Reninghelst.	19/08/1917	24/08/1917
War Diary	Eperlecques	25/08/1917	30/08/1917
War Diary	Fremicourt.	31/08/1917	30/09/1917
Operation(al) Order(s)	56th Divisional Engineers' Order No. 119.	01/09/1917	01/09/1917
Miscellaneous	Amendment to 56th Divisional Engineers' Order No. 119.	03/09/1917	03/09/1917
War Diary	Fremicourt	14/10/1917	16/10/1917
War Diary	Fremicourt	01/11/1917	23/11/1917
Miscellaneous	H.Q. "G" 56th Divn.	14/12/1917	14/12/1917
War Diary	Fremicourt	03/12/1917	03/12/1917
War Diary	Fosseux	05/12/1917	05/12/1917
War Diary	G3b74	08/12/1917	20/12/1917
War Diary	G3b74 (Sheet 51B)	02/01/1918	09/01/1918
War Diary	A20d43	10/01/1918	29/01/1918
Heading	War Diary Headquarters, Royal Engineers, 56th Division. March 1918		
War Diary	G3b.7.4	01/03/1918	30/03/1918
Heading	56th Divisional Engineers C.R.E. 56th Division April 1918.		
War Diary	ACQ	01/04/1918	08/04/1918
War Diary	Berneville	23/04/1918	23/04/1918
War Diary	Berneville	08/04/1918	10/05/1918
War Diary	Warlus	11/05/1918	14/07/1918
War Diary	Beugin	15/07/1918	23/07/1918
War Diary	Bajus	18/07/1918	31/07/1918
War Diary		23/07/1918	23/07/1918
War Diary	Bajus	01/08/1918	01/08/1918
War Diary	Warlus	18/08/1918	18/08/1918
War Diary	Le Cauroy	22/08/1918	22/08/1918
War Diary	Bavincourt	24/08/1918	24/08/1918
War Diary	Blaireville Quarry	27/08/1918	27/08/1918
Heading	War Diary September 1918 56th Divisional Engineers Headquarters		
War Diary	Boisleux St. Marc.	01/09/1918	01/09/1918
War Diary	Les Fosses Farm.	09/09/1918	09/09/1918
War Diary	Villers Les Cagnicourt.	26/09/1918	30/09/1918
Miscellaneous	C.E. XXIInd. Corps No. E.B. 724.	28/09/1918	28/09/1918
Miscellaneous	O.C. 512th (London) Fd. Co. R.E.	05/10/1918	05/10/1918
Miscellaneous	Stock Report-Showing Material on hand at		
Miscellaneous	First Army No. 2894	04/10/1918	04/10/1918
Miscellaneous	G.H.Q. 2/10/18.	03/10/1918	03/10/1918

Type	Description	Start	End
Miscellaneous		23/06/1917	23/06/1917
Miscellaneous	E., XXIInd Corps.	28/09/1918	28/09/1918
War Diary	Villers Les Cagnicourt.	01/10/1918	15/10/1918
Miscellaneous	C.R.E. 56th Division. Account of operations carried out by Royal Engineers of the 56th Division, and Pioneers-Nov. 2nd to 11th 1918.	15/11/1918	15/11/1918
War Diary		01/11/1916	28/11/1916
War Diary	Harvengt.	01/12/1918	31/12/1918
Heading	56th Divnl Engineers War Diary January 1919 Vol 46		
War Diary	Harvengt	01/01/1919	31/01/1919
Heading	War Diary February 1919. 56th Divnl. Engineers Vol 47		
War Diary	Harvengt.	01/02/1919	29/03/1919
War Diary	Quaregnon.	29/03/1919	30/04/1919
War Diary		07/04/1919	08/04/1919
War Diary	Quaregnon	01/05/1919	18/05/1919

WO 95/2939/1

56TH DIVISION

C. R. E.
FEB 1916 – MAY 1919

Army Form C. 2118.

WAR DIARY
or
INTELLIGENCE SUMMARY.
(Erase heading not required.)

Instructions regarding War Diaries and Intelligence Summaries are contained in F. S. Regs., Part II. and the Staff Manual respectively. Title pages will be prepared in manuscript.

H.Q. 56th Divl. E.N.G.S.

Place	Date	Hour	Summary of Events and Information	Remarks and references to Appendices
HALLENCOURT	5.2.16		C.R.E. appointed to 56th Div. Arrived at HALLENCOURT evening of 5th	
	6.2.16		Part of H.Q. Staff arrived on same date	
	7.2.16		No news of companies or troops.	
	8.2.16		"	
	9.2.16		Infantry commenced arrival	
	10.2.16		Infantry arrived	
	11.2.16		"	
	12.2.16		"	
	13.2.16		Train arrived. Pioneer regt arriving	
	14.2.16		Taking over Offices & took C.R.E. by 55th Div.	
	16.2.16		Borrowed a Cart Horse on a.c. Captain from Pioneers and 4th Puthead Survey arrived for office	
	16.2.16		Motor Bicycle and Sidecar arrived at 3600 per Divn. Motor bicycles arrived	
	17.2.16		Capt. D.H. Innes R.E. in charge of Divl. workshops arrived. In 5 m.c. @ 140/p.w. 8 m.c. 800 sides	
	18.2.16			
	19.2.16		Purchase 2 cavalry n.c.o. + officer	

Army Form C. 2118.

WAR DIARY
or
INTELLIGENCE SUMMARY.
(Erase heading not required.)

H.Qrs 56th Divl. Engrs.

Instructions regarding War Diaries and Intelligence Summaries are contained in F. S. Regs., Part II. and the Staff Manual respectively. Title pages will be prepared in manuscript.

Place	Date	Hour	Summary of Events and Information	Remarks and references to Appendices
HALLENCOURT	20/2/16		Some time spent in fitting H.Q. Sr Offrs in with mess & collecting gear made for G.S. wagons for Biscs - Bedding materials etc	
"	21/2/16			
"	22/2/16			Snow + frost
"	23/2/16			"
"	24/2/16		1/1st 2/2nd Sections fired Guard. Division received orders to prepare to move on the following day. Orders to move postponed for 24 hrs delay.	
"	25/2/16		Billets were paid up & Stores packed ready to move. Orders received for Division to move N.E. on the 27th. 167th Brigade group & 2/2nd Coy to 168th Brigade group	About 5" snow fallen still freezing - roads v. slippery.
"	26/2/16		Hd. Qr. Batpenelle attached to 2/2 Coy for the move. C.R.E. walked with 2/1st Coy at HOCQUINCOURT. C.R.E. went to ABBEVILLE in the afternoon to draw moneys. Offrs packed up ready to move in the morning.	Snow cut in about 12 mm.
DOMART	27/2/16		Hd. Qr. moved off at 10.15 A.M. & arrived at DOMART at about 3 P.M. Orders received for march to DOULLENS next day.	Some snow + Rain
"	28/2/16		Orders for move postponed. C.R.E. & Adj. visited 2/2nd Field Coy. at	

T.134. Wt. W708-776. 50000. 4/15. Sir J.C. & S.

Army Form C. 2118.

WAR DIARY
or
INTELLIGENCE SUMMARY.
(Erase heading not required.)

H.Qrs. 56th Divisional Engrs

Place	Date	Hour	Summary of Events and Information	Remarks and references to Appendices
DOMART	28/2/16		Bougons > The 2/1st Field Coy at BERTEAUCOURT - They had apparently managed the move quite well.	Snow - men frozen 3 men'd round
	29/2		No orders to move received	all snow drifts

Jas Foster
LtCol RE
CRE 56th Div

Army Form C. 2118.

WAR DIARY
or
INTELLIGENCE SUMMARY.
(Erase heading not required.)

HQ 3rd 58th Divisional Engrs

Place	Date	Hour	Summary of Events and Information	Remarks and references to Appendices
DOMART	1/3/16		Information received. Division notified to move for five or six days. Field Coys asked to send in programmes for Train instructional courses.	Snow reported
"	2/3/16		Seven drivers & 1 sapper reported. Arrived to Divl Eng HQ	" " "
"	3/3/16		C.Q.M.S. DESMOND joined the Division as acting R.S.M. C.R.E left for Bus to visit Offrs Transfer of 48th Division. M"	Some snow"
"	4/3/16		BOUQUET joined Hd Qr Divl Eng, an interview Adj visited 2/3 Coy to discuss "French" movement	Bright & cold
"	5/3/16		Adj went to AMIENS to make purchases & visited the Annexe Section de Camouflage	"
"	6/3/16		C.R.E returned from BUS	"
"	7/3/16		Sgt Steward joined Division as Engineer Clerk	Rain
"	8/3/16		No materials or transport available	
"	9/3/16			
"	10/3/16		Adj visited 2/1st 2d Coy	
"	11/3/16		Orders received to march to DOULLENS on following day	
DOULLENS	12/3/16		Divl Eng HQ moved off at 8.45 AM & arrived at DOULLENS about	

Army Form C. 2118.

WAR DIARY
or
INTELLIGENCE SUMMARY.
(Erase heading not required.)

H.Q. 56th Divn R.E.

Place	Date	Hour	Summary of Events and Information	Remarks and references to Appendices
DOULLENS	12.3.16		Arrived 3 p.m. Billeted in Rue d'Arras.	Weather Warm & Fine.
	13.3.16		Adjutant visited MONDICOURT to enquire as to Stores.	
	14.3.16		Orders received to Move on 17th. Lieut Fraser S.J.C. (R.A.M.C) joined as M.O.	
	15.3.16		C.R.E. visited proposed new Divisional area & Headquarters area with Staff to assist in fixing sites of R.E. Stores, Dump, & Workshops & to gain an idea of R.E work necessary.	
	16.3.16		Adjutant visited MONDICOURT & purchased timber. Enquiries made as to stores of timber available.	
LE COUROY	17.3.16		Moved to LE COUROY. Arrived 3 p.m. 1 Casualty (Driver thrown from Horse). Timber purchased on 16th (5 tons) brought up & Stores & Material removed from Longpré Dump to HALLENCOURT DUMP. (NOTE - For H.Q. R.E. a G.S. Wagon is more serviceable than a G.S. limber. It can be packed easier, holds more, & only requires same number of Horses. The limber forming part of A.S.C. train is not commendable as R.E Stores which may be urgently required are packed with & the Train may be parked at a distance)	Weather Dull. Roads - good.
	18.3.16		Opened R.E. Dump. System of issuing stores circulated to all concerned. Found it necessary to have 4 - 3ton lorries Question of drawing stores from R.E. Parks gone into. Obtained these from D.A.C. for drawing up Stores.	

Army Form C. 2118.

WAR DIARY
or
INTELLIGENCE SUMMARY.
(Erase heading not required.)

H.Q. 56th Divn R.E.

Instructions regarding War Diaries and Intelligence Summaries are contained in F. S. Regs., Part II. and the Staff Manual respectively. Title pages will be prepared in manuscript.

Place	Date	Hour	Summary of Events and Information	Remarks and references to Appendices
				Weather
LE COUROY	19.3.16		C.R.E visited Divisional Area - selected sites for Baths & Laundry - Allotment of Stores made & issued.	Rain at frequent intervals
	20.3.16		Commenced issuing Stores. Drew out specifications for standardizing (a) Latrines (b) Water Troughs (c) Tables - Portability of each article being considered essential. Plans sent X.R. (App B) Telephone installed. Horse cast by A.V.C (Leaving 5 instead of 7)	"
	21.3.16		2 Horses cast by A.V.C (leaving 3 instead of 7) - Consultation with Officers of Field Companies as to programme of works.	"
	22.3.16		C.R.E. visited Park at MONDICOURT & district to ascertain stores available for works necessary in this area - Plans for Divisional Laundry settled.	"
	23.3.16		C.R.E. visited PREVENT to try & arrange for carriage of Stores from new R.E. Park by Railway	"
	24.3.16		Adjutant visited GRAND ROULLECOURT & WARLUZEL to try & buy Stores (notably canvas) - none available - Purchased rolling machine & anvil - Also visited AVESNES-LE-COMTE & Corps Headquarters.	"
	25.3.16		Consultation with C.E. 6th Corps - Following matters discussed & encamped: Horse-Standings Divisional Baths - Laundry - Saw Mill.	"

Army Form C. 2118.

WAR DIARY
or
INTELLIGENCE SUMMARY.
(Erase heading not required.)

Instructions regarding War Diaries and Intelligence Summaries are contained in F. S. Regs., Part II. and the Staff Manual respectively. Title pages will be prepared in manuscript.

Place	Date	Hour	Summary of Events and Information	Remarks and references to Appendices
LE COUROY	26.3.16		Issued Instructions to 2/1 London Fd. Coy to move to Front Line. Found impossible for whole Coy to be billeted in DUISSANS. Arranged for two Sections to go to ARRAS. Decided to move last named Sections by Motor Transport. Two Sections of 2/2 London Fd Coy instructed to take over duties of 2/1 Company. Weekly allotment of R.E. Stores made & issued. Letter as to method of issuing circulated to Units concerned.	
"	27.3.16 6.0 am		Two Sections 2/1 Coy commenced move. Remainder marched. Move successfull. Two Sections of 2/2 Coy moved to HONVAL. Made arrangements for purchasing bricks at 21 frs per 1000 at MUNCHEAUX (Note. This arrangement was subsequently marred by Unit from another Division purchasing at Frs.25 per 1000. It seems essential that purchases for R.E. Works should be centralized as directly more than one purchaser is found a cheap market is spoilt.) Instructions issued by H.Q. for Horse Standings to be made where immediately necessary. Type plan drawn up & approved.	
"	28.3.16		Consultation with C.E. 6th Corps on R.E. Works generally. Visited areas occupied by 2/1st Company. Drew out rough sketch of M.G. Emplacement for them to	

Army Form C. 2118

H.Q. 57th Divl. R.E.

WAR DIARY or INTELLIGENCE SUMMARY.

(Erase heading not required.)

Instructions regarding War Diaries and Intelligence Summaries are contained in F.S. Regs., Part II. and the Staff Manual respectively. Title pages will be prepared in manuscript.

Place	Date	Hour	Summary of Events and Information	Remarks and references to Appendices
LE CAUROY	28.3.18		To make. (Appendix) Agreement for land for 161st Brigade Baths passed for approval	
"	29.3.18		As it was found impossible to get immediate supplies of cut timber – visited AVESNES-LE-COMTE arranged to hire sawmill there – also arranged to buy trees. D.H.Q. decided that screens no longer necessary for horse standings.	
"	30.3.18		Minor repairs of roads on 161st Brigade Area carried out. Large quantity of notice boards for arable fields made & issued. Sketch issued to Units showing type of horse standings desirable. Purchased circular & hand saw – engine & fittings for 3000 Francs for use in connection with carpenters shop & for cutting up planks from AVESNES mill.	
"	31.3.18		Conference with Staff Captain R.A. as to devising portable bridge for getting guns across trenches – Arranged for experiments in connection with same.	
	Note		Each day 4 motor lorries left LE CAUROY & brought up all available stores from R.E. Parks – The use of these lorries was found to be of great assistance in getting materials. In fact they are indispensable	

T.134. Wt. W708-776. 500000. 4/15. Sir J.C. & S.

Army Form C. 2118.

WAR DIARY
or
INTELLIGENCE SUMMARY.

(Erase heading not required.)

CRE. 56 D

Place	Date	Hour	Summary of Events and Information	Remarks and references to Appendices
LE CAUROY	1.4.16		Sawmill purchased on 31-3-16 erected in LE CAUROY by Section of 2/2 Field Co. No hitch in erection. Arrangements made for further purchases of longe trees to be cut at AVESNES. Question of transport again a difficulty. Borrowed horses for timber cart from Train Transport.	
	2.4.16		Clearing area	
	3.4.16		ditto	
	4.4.16		ditto. C.R.E. left for England on Leave.	
	5.4.16		ditto	
	6.4.16		ditto. Q.M.S. Hartnell passed from C.E. 6th Corps for duty as F/W.	
	7.4.16		ditto	
	8.4.16		"	
	9.4.16		" C.R.E. returned from leave. 2/2 London Field Co relieved 2/1 London Field Co in front line. ARRAS.	
	10.4.16			

Army Form C. 2118.

WAR DIARY
or
INTELLIGENCE SUMMARY.
(Erase heading not required.)

Place	Date	Hour	Summary of Events and Information	Remarks and references to Appendices
LE CAUROY	11.4.16		Cleaning area	
	12.4.16		ditto	
	13.4.16		Section of 2/1 London Field Co under Lieut W. Sharkis arrived & took over works in H.Q. Area.	
	14.4.16		Cleaning area	
	15.4.16		ditto	
	16.4.16		ditto C.R.E. left for AUXI-LE-CHATEAU for C.O's conference	
	17.4.16		ditto	
	18.4.16		Conference with Staff Captain R.A. as to types of M.G. Emplacements.	
	19.4.16		Adjutant lectured to Div: School on defence of a village.	
	20.4.16		Cleaning area.	
	21.4.16		C.E. VI Corps called & made enquiries as to works in progress about Survey of River Le Conche commenced at MAGNICOURT under direction of M.O undertaken with view to ascertaining supply & quality of water	

Army Form C. 2118.

WAR DIARY
or
INTELLIGENCE SUMMARY.
(Erase heading not required.)

Instructions regarding War Diaries and Intelligence Summaries are contained in F.S. Regs., Part II. and the Staff Manual respectively. Title pages will be prepared in manuscript.

Place	Date	Hour	Summary of Events and Information	Remarks and references to Appendices
LE CAURON	22.4.16		Test by R.A. of 1st portable Bridge - Time taken in getting guns across French 15 minutes.	
	23.4.16		Survey of River Le Conche (to REBREUVE) - completed. C.R.E. returned from conference	
	24.4.16		Report on river completed - copies to Div. H.Q. & A.D.M.S. Adjutant granted leave to England	
	25.4.16		Cleaning area	
	26.4.16		Cleaning area - 11pm Received telegram that EDINBURGH Fd Co would arrive tomorrow	
	27.4.16		Cleaning area. Pt of Edinburgh Field Co arrived - 167 - without transport - the wagons having been left at MARSEILLES owing to lack of railway transport - the mounted section left at ABBEVILLE to get horses.	
ROUM	28.4.16		Test of revised type Portable Artillery Bridge carried out by R.F.A. Gun, limber and teams crossed successfully. Time taken to fix bridge, cross trench and get gun	

Army Form C. 2118.

WAR DIARY
or
INTELLIGENCE SUMMARY.
(Erase heading not required.)

Instructions regarding War Diaries and Intelligence Summaries are contained in F. S. Regs., Part II. and the Staff Manual respectively. Title pages will be prepared in manuscript.

Place	Date	Hour	Summary of Events and Information	Remarks and references to Appendices
LE CAUROY	28.4.16		into position for firing – 10 minutes (Type Plan 6a)	Appendix A
	29.4.16		C.R.E. attended display at Divisional School of various trench devices etc. Portable Infantry Bridge (Type Plan 4) – Dugout (Type Plan 8) Superscope (Type Plan 9) Improvement of Edinburgh field tested & found satisfactory	B.C. + D
	29.9.16 30.9.16		cleaning area – The month was mainly taken up in improving Area – erecting baths at BERLEN-COURT and REBREUVE – establishing Divl. Laundries at AVESNES-LE-COMTE & PREVENT. also providing water troughs – drinking stations for troops on the march – Incinerators – Latrines etc.	

1st May 1916.

J. S. Gordon
Lieut. Colo. R.E.
C.R.E. 56th Division.

Army Form C. 2118.

WAR DIARY
or
INTELLIGENCE SUMMARY.
(Erase heading not required.)

May 1916
H.Q. 56th Div² ⁷ʳ

Instructions regarding War Diaries and Intelligence Summaries are contained in F.S. Regs., Part II. and the Staff Manual respectively. Title pages will be prepared in manuscript.

Place	Date	Hour	Summary of Events and Information	Remarks and references to Appendices
LE CAUROY	1.5.16		Survey (Preliminary) of Light Railway FIREVENT to AVESNES-LE-COMTE commenced with view to its being used for carriage of stores & so lighten traffic on road to ARRAS.	Weather fine
		11.30 p.m.	Notification received that Division would shortly move into VII Corps Area (D.O. N° 5) & that if Edinburgh Field C° would come under orders of G.O.C. R.A. on completion of move.	
"	2.5.16		Above survey continued. Arrangements put in hand for leaving Area. C.R.E. visited new area with G.S.O.¹ 167th Copy Brigade order N° 7	
		8 p.m.	Div. Order N° 6 received	
"	3.5.16		Completed Report on Light Railway. Preparing data for Corps distribution return. 167th Copy Div. Order N° 7 received	Appendix A
		6 p.m.	Received Brigade Order N° 6	
"	4.5.16		Dismantling Saw mill & removing same to new area. Found that large quantity of stores were returned at last moment before move by many units.	
"	5.5.16		Moved Office from LE CAUROY to HENU - used motor lorry - left 1.30 p.m. arrived 3.30 p.m. Found on arrival that rooms allotted for Office had been	
HENU				

Army Form C. 2118

WAR DIARY
or
INTELLIGENCE SUMMARY.
(Erase heading not required.)

Instructions regarding War Diaries and Intelligence Summaries are contained in F. S. Regs., Part II. and the Staff Manual respectively. Title pages will be prepared in manuscript.

Place	Date	Hour	Summary of Events and Information	Remarks and references to Appendices
HENU	5.5.16		re-allotted - Office in lorry over-night	
"	6.5.16		Secured offices - work commenced. Workshop on main PAS - HENU road opened. Portable saw-bench installed. Temporary stores dump opened at rear of shops - Made arrangements for hiring steam saw for log-cutting - S/o London Terr. arrived.	
"	7.5.16		Telephone installed. Arrangements made for French map (20 sft to 1 mile) to be made in office - to be compiled from Ordnance Map & Aeroplane photographs.	
"	8.5.16		C.R.E. attended conference called by G.O.C. Division. Adjutant visited BAYENCOURT - fixed site for Dump. Stores transferred there by motor lorry from temporary dump at HENU. Carpenters & Blacksmiths by working in HENU under 2/c N° 4 Section 2/2 London Field C°.	
"	9.5.16		C.R.E. visited trenches with Brig General 169th Brigade. Instructions issued for 2 sections 2/2 London Field C° to move into trenches. Lefthalf of 3rd Bridging Train arrived	
"	10.5.16		C.R.E. showed again cook by A.V.C. Found that amount of work required in Front line was more than could possibly be got through by Section at Workshops - Application to D.H.Q. for rough carpenters to be attached.	

Army Form C. 2118

WAR DIARY
or
INTELLIGENCE SUMMARY.
(Erase heading not required.)

C.R.E.

Instructions regarding War Diaries and Intelligence Summaries are contained in F.S. Regs., Part II. and the Staff Manual respectively. Title pages will be prepared in manuscript.

Place: HENU 56th Div (1/3)

Date	Hour	Summary of Events and Information	Remarks and references to Appendices
			Weather
HENU 10.5.16		16 Rough Carpenters from Brigades joined for work at Shop.	Showery Dull
11.5.16		10 " " " " " "	"
12.5.16		Enlarged plan made of German trenches around GOMMECOURT WOOD. Conference with O. cs to laying out facsimile trenches.	
13.5.16		C.R.E. went to HALLOY - met there Brig. Gen. & Brigade Major - laid out approximately 1000 yards facsimile enemy trench for practice work.	Very Wet
14.5.16		Laying out of above system of trenches completed - Infantry started digging on them. C.R.E. had conference with C.E. VII Corps - matters discussed Water supply - maintenance of roads - work to be done in front line & informed him of methods & work in progress.	
15.5.16		Adjutant visited Damp - Further considering question of upkeep of roads & supply of installing etc.	Wet
16.5.16		Received report of 4 casualties 2/2 London T.C. - 2 killed 2 wounded. Found could not turn out works as quickly as desired owing to lack of skilled labour.	Warm & fine
17.5.16		C.R.E. visited front line trenches to see progress being made by Sections	"

Army Form C. 2118

WAR DIARY
or
INTELLIGENCE SUMMARY.
(Erase heading not required.)

Place	Date	Hour	Summary of Events and Information	Remarks and references to Appendices
HENU	17.5.16		Adjutants horse cast by A.V.C.	Weather FINE
	18.5.16		C.R.E. visited C.E. VII Corps. Conference on roads & works supply, informing him of progress of works on hand.	"
	19.5.16		Received D.O. No 9 advising movement of Brigades. Got out for C.E. list of villages, men & horses billetted in same & schedule of requirements for supply of water. C.R.E. & Adjutant visited trenches, inspected works in progress & discussed with 7.S. Companies their requirements and regarding labour & materials.	"
		8.45 pm	Received Veller setting out system of which for trench work.	"
	20.5.16		Preliminary survey made of HEBUTERNE for Officers Trench Snap.	"
	21.5.16		Plans prepared for laying out at HALLOY of further enemy trenches for practice work.	"
	22.5.16		Commenced laying out of above trenches.	"
	23.5.16		Completed same. C.R.E. visited HEBUTERNE & inspected works on hand.	"
	24.5.16		Received from D.H.Q. further air photos for compiling Officers Trench map.	"

WAR DIARY
or
"INTELLIGENCE SUMMARY."
(Erase heading not required.)

Army Form C. 2118.

Place	Date	Hour	Summary of Events and Information	Remarks and references to Appendices
HENU	25.5.16		Further work on laying out at HALLOY of practice trenches	
	26.5.16		New trench in advance of existing front line dug & completed C.R.E. visited HEBUTERNE inspected new work - also inspected progress of other work	
	27.5.16		Routine work	
	28.5.16		" "	
	29.5.16		" "	
	30.5.16		" "	

56th Division.

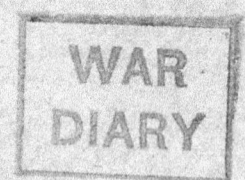

C. R. E.

56th DIVISIONAL ENGINEERS.

JUNE 1916

Appendices 1 to 8.

Army Form C.

WAR DIARY
or
INTELLIGENCE SUMMARY
(Erase heading not required.)

Instructions regarding War Diaries and Intelligence Summaries are contained in F.S. Regs., Part II. and the Staff Manual respectively. Title Pages will be prepared in manuscript.

Place	Date	Hour	Summary of Events and Information	Remarks and references to Appendices
HENU	June 1st 1916		Made arrangements for working of Quarry COIGNEUX to procure metal for roads. Star Drill at HEBUTERNE moved away by C.E. Corps. Question of water supply there gone into & orders issued 1/6 Field Company as to work to be done	
	June 2nd		C.R.E. visited trenches to note progress of work. 1800 yards of facsimile enemy trench laid out at HALLOY for practice for the Brigades which it was anticipated would take part in any attack. Took over roads in forward area & made arrangements for work thereon. Adjutant returned from leave to England.	
	" 3rd		H.Q. & Transport of Edinburgh Field Co ordered to move to MONDICOURT. To establish Artillery dump there	
	" 4th		Working out details for construction of Bomb. store at BAYENCOURT by Pioneers. Relieved "SENTINEL" forcing jack from 7th CORPS.	Weather Showery
	" 5		Making arrangements for demonstration of wire cutting by means of "BANGALORE" Torpedoes including training by Adjutant of sappers in filling Torpedoes with Ammonal – fusing etc.	

WAR DIARY or INTELLIGENCE SUMMARY

Army Form C.2118

(Erase heading not required.)

Place	Date	Hour	Summary of Events and Information	Remarks and references to Appendices
HENU	1916 JUNE 5		Practice carried out with "SENTINEL" forcing jack	Weather
"	6		Orders issued for 1 Officer & 1 N.C.O from each Company to attend forcing jack demonstration by 6th Corps.	"FINE
"	7		Report on cellars at HEBUTERNE giving thicknesses of overhead cover, walls etc prepared and sent to C.E. 7th Corps. 1 hour rest.	"RAINY
"	7		Received our photos showing new front trench. New work plotted on to trench map.	Rain all day
"	8		Officers & N.C.O's attended 6th Corps demonstration with forcing jack	Heavy rain all day
"	9		Instructions received for small dug-outs to be constructed - Frames for same sent in hand at workshop.	Showery
"	10		Instructions received that intended Recom Sap would not be made 2 Horses arrived	Fine

Army Form C. 2118

WAR DIARY
or
INTELLIGENCE SUMMARY
(Erase heading not required.)

Instructions regarding War Diaries and Intelligence Summaries are contained in F. S. Regs., Part II. and the Staff Manual respectively. Title Pages will be prepared in manuscript.

56th Division C.R.E.

Place	Date	Hour	Summary of Events and Information	Remarks and references to Appendices
HENU	1916 June 10		Application made to Div. H.Q. for extra subalterns for each Field Co. Received intimation from Corps that no stone could be supplied. Demonstration of "Fumite" Bomb held at HALLOY practice trenches.	Weather - Wet
	" 11		Demonstration of Traverse destroying by Ammonal charges given (see Report No 1.) Received notification that sand now available for R.E. work. Report received of work done to roads.	Weather - Fair Appendix 1
	" 12		Issued instructions to 2/1st and 2/2nd Field Companies to make reconnaissance of roads near new front line to ascertain work necessary to put roads into walkable condition in view of any possible advance.	"
	" 13		Routine work.	"
	" 14		Received from D.H.Q. the preliminary instructions for forthcoming operations - worked out details of labour required and tasks to be accomplished - and got out general scheme for employment of R.E.'s during the intermediate period - sent notes to problems which might arise in the event of an advance. Prepared note of R.E. Stores to be placed in	

1875 Wt. W593/826 1,000,000 4/15 J.B.C. & A. A.D.S.S./Forms/C. 2118.

WAR DIARY
or
INTELLIGENCE SUMMARY
(Erase heading not required.)

Army Form C. 2118

Place	Date	Hour	Summary of Events and Information	Remarks and references to Appendices
HENU	1918 June 14		advanced Brigade Dumps. Received from Div. H.Q. "Preliminary Instructions for 58th Division". Received reports of 2/1st and 2/2nd Companies on roads & work required thereon in the event of an advance.	Weather: Wet
	" 15		Conference with Field Company Officers - informing them of work which would be expected of their Companies and giving them here outline of intended operations - Enlarged trench map of Divisional Area completed. Interviewed Brig: General Commanding 168th Infantry Brigade with reference to R.E. arrangements, discussing same at length & certain alterations were suggested in regard to the position of the advanced trench.	Appendix 2
	" 16		Prepared lists of proposed moves of the 12 sections of the Companies up to 24th June. Interviewed Major Glover 3rd London Reg:t & Major Samuel 1st London Reg:t who were to be in charge of parties to work on saps forward to enemy line & entrusted to them that Lewis gunners working thereon. Received amendment to Div. H.Q. "Preliminary instructions". 2nd Lieut: Aitkin Edinburgh Field C.- sick to Hospital.	"Fine

WAR DIARY or INTELLIGENCE SUMMARY

Army Form C 2118

C.R.E.

Instructions regarding War Diaries and Intelligence Summaries are contained in F.S. Regs., Part II. and the Staff Manual respectively. Title Pages will be prepared in manuscript.

(Erase heading not required.)

Place	Date	Hour	Summary of Events and Information	Remarks and references to Appendices
HENU	1916 June 11		Issued letter to above Officers with copy of map showing proposed position of communication trenches and with instructions	Appendix 3
			Attended practice attack at HALLOY.	Weather fine
			German aeroplane raiding party (9 machines) crossed office going in direction of PAS.	
			Table of working party required for forward C.T.'s sent to 167th Bde.	
			Received Divisional Order No. 12.	Appendix 4
			Worked out table of labour required on proposed forward C.T.'s.	
			Carried out demonstration for G.O.C. and staff of new netting by Wootton Pull	Appendix 5
	..18		means of Bangalore Torpedoes.	
			Orders issued to Edinburgh Field Co. in regard to work to be done on roads & barricades.	Appendix 6
			Received Divisional Order No. 13.	
			Details issued to Officers i/c working parties as to work on forward C.T.'s on the night of 19th.	
		11 p.m.	Received telegram that digging of forward C.T.'s would be postponed from night 19th/20th to the night of 21st/22nd.	

WAR DIARY
or
INTELLIGENCE SUMMARY
(Erase heading not required.)

Army Form C.

Instructions regarding War Diaries and Intelligence Summaries are contained in F.S. Regs., Part II. and the Staff Manual respectively. Title Pages will be prepared in manuscript.

Place	Date	Hour	Summary of Events and Information	Remarks and references to Appendices
HEINU	1916 JUNE 19th		Issued further instructions to Major Samuel 1st London Regt & Major Glover 3rd London Regiment in regard to digging forward C.T.s. Inspection made of trenches in Divisional Area by G.O.C. VII Corps.	Weather fine. Appendix 1
	" 20		Routine work.	Weather "
	" 21		Received from D.H.Q. Instructions for Preliminary Period. Schedule of R.E. arrangements. " " Preliminary administrative instructions. Survey of HEBUTERNE forward trenches made for purpose of maps. Received instructions that one of the proposed C.T.s would not be dug. Orders issued to Officers i/c Working Parties accordingly. Major O.R.B. Johnstone 2/1 London Field Co recalled to England.	"
	" 22		Received Further Preliminary Administrative Instructions in continuation of those received 17-6-18. Received Schedule of method of signal communications during active operations. Copy of trench map made for C.R.A.	"

Army Form C.2

WAR DIARY
or
INTELLIGENCE SUMMARY

(Erase heading not required.)

Instructions regarding War Diaries and Intelligence Summaries are contained in F.S. Regs., Part II. and the Staff Manual respectively. Title Pages will be prepared in manuscript.

Place	Date	Hour	Summary of Events and Information	Remarks and references to Appendices
HENU	1916 June 23		Intimation received that to-morrow would be "Y" day. Copy of trench map made for C.E. Corps showing R.E. depots + dumps. Received intimation that smoke discharges would be made in co-operation with artillery bombardments. Issued instructions to 2/1st & 2/2nd Edinburgh Field Co giving the positions of the Companies during the offensive.	Heavy Storm
	" 24		Received Divl. Orders Nº 14 and 15. Issued table showing allocation of R.E. and Pioneers for "Z" day i.e. day of attack.	Showery
	" 25		Received instructions that notice boards for traffic roads used at night should be painted with luminous paint. 8 German aeroplanes crossed HENU in direction of PAS. Lieut H.F. Williamson - Edinburgh Field Co wounded + evacuated.	Fine
	" 26		Received schedule of operations for motor machine gun battery & its intended use. Issued orders to 1/1 Edinburgh Field Co to report return roads cleaned & fit for motor cycles with side cars. Received instructions to move 3 sections 2/1st London Field Co and 2 Sections 2/2 London Field Co to SAILLY at midnight Y/Z night. Orders issued accordingly.	Wet

Army Form C.2118

WAR DIARY
or
INTELLIGENCE SUMMARY
(Erase heading not required.)

Place	Date	Hour	Summary of Events and Information	Remarks and references to Appendices
HENU	1916 June 26		Received amendments to methods of signal communications. Issued instructions to the 3 Companies in regard to their work during the next few days and generally. Received from Div. H.Q. "Instructions as to clearing the Battlefield" Capt. D.G. Smith Edinburgh To C. - Died from Wounds received.	Appendix B
	" 27.		All R.E. arrangements complete for proposed attack on German lines. Orders issued to Edinburgh Field Co in regard to roads.	
	" 28		C.R.E. moved to Advanced Divisional Headquarters SOUASTRE - on arrival found that attack had been postponed by 48 hours - had to return to HENU office. Received instructions that moves ordered in D.O. N°14 would be postponed by 48 hours - Received D.O. N°16 - Notified Companies of postponement. Supply of BANGALORE Torpedoes prepared.	

WAR DIARY
or
INTELLIGENCE SUMMARY

(Erase heading not required.)

Army Form C 2

Place	Date	Hour	Summary of Events and Information	Remarks and references to Appendices
HENU	1916 June 29		Conference with C.E. topo on R.E arrangements - made & discussing same with him.	
	" 30		Capt R. Annan 2/1 London Field Co. to hospital sick. Received orders that BANGALORE torpedo parties would be required tonight - arranged details - issued instructions to 2/1st & 2/2nd Field Companies to provide torpedo parties. Orders issued to Companies to move tonight. C.R.E. moved to Advanced Div. H.Q 23rd.	

Note Generally

The past month was one of great activity so far as R.E work & personnel were concerned. In addition to the drawing of stores & making of trench articles (e.g. trench elements, trench hurdles etc) for normal requirements & the ordinary work of the area - arrangements had to be made to have a sufficient supply of trench ladders & portable artillery bridges available for the attack. All demands of Division and Brigades were met. It was also necessary to

Army Form C.2118

WAR DIARY
or
INTELLIGENCE SUMMARY
(Erase heading not required.)

Instructions regarding War Diaries and Intelligence Summaries are contained in F.S. Regs., Part II. and the Staff Manual respectively. Title Pages will be prepared in manuscript.

56th Division

Place	Date	Hour	Summary of Events and Information	Remarks and references to Appendices
HENU			Notes Generally con: establish Advanced Dumps of R.E. materials for use in case of an advance which entailed considerable extra labour — These stores were all done up in man-loads which were, if the attack were successful, to be man handled to pre-arranged spots. I think that in regard to Divisional Units there should be a reserve of R.E. Officers available at the Base as somewhere reinforcements for each Divisional Engineers. They could be usefully employed there on the various hutting & other camp works which are always in progress — In regard to the attack the Companies under my command I found that on the eve of the attack I was left with the following Officers:— Edinburgh Field Co. .... Major & 4 subalterns 2/1 London .... " " " " " 2/2 " .... " " " " " .... Major & 4 subalterns Having regard to the organisation of a Field Co. Officers on a total of 18 would have considerable effect on the work and the effectiveness of the Company	

J.A. Foster
Lt Col R.E.
C.R.E. 56th Division

KEY TO TRENCH MAP

Trenches .... shewn	
Parapets and Parados	
Probable location of dug-outs or shelters in trenches the extra width of parapet and parados denoting spare earth	
Dug-outs and shelters other than in line of trenches	
Low wire entanglements	
High wire entanglements	
Footpaths	
Larger tracks than footpaths	
Roads	
Trees and woods	
Sunken roads	
Houses and buildings	
Rifle Pits	
Contour lines	
Hedges	
Trench tramway	

SECRET. NO.

Office of the C.R.E.
56th Divisional Engineers.

Appendix (1)

Cartridges for the purpose of destroying traverses and blocking enemy trenches.

These cartridges may be employed as follows :-

An auger hole 5' deep is made by means of a screw picket near the bottom of the trench at the shoulder of the traverse to be destroyed.

The cartridge is then pushed home and tamped when it is ready for exploding.

The above operation requires 2 men and takes about 10 minutes

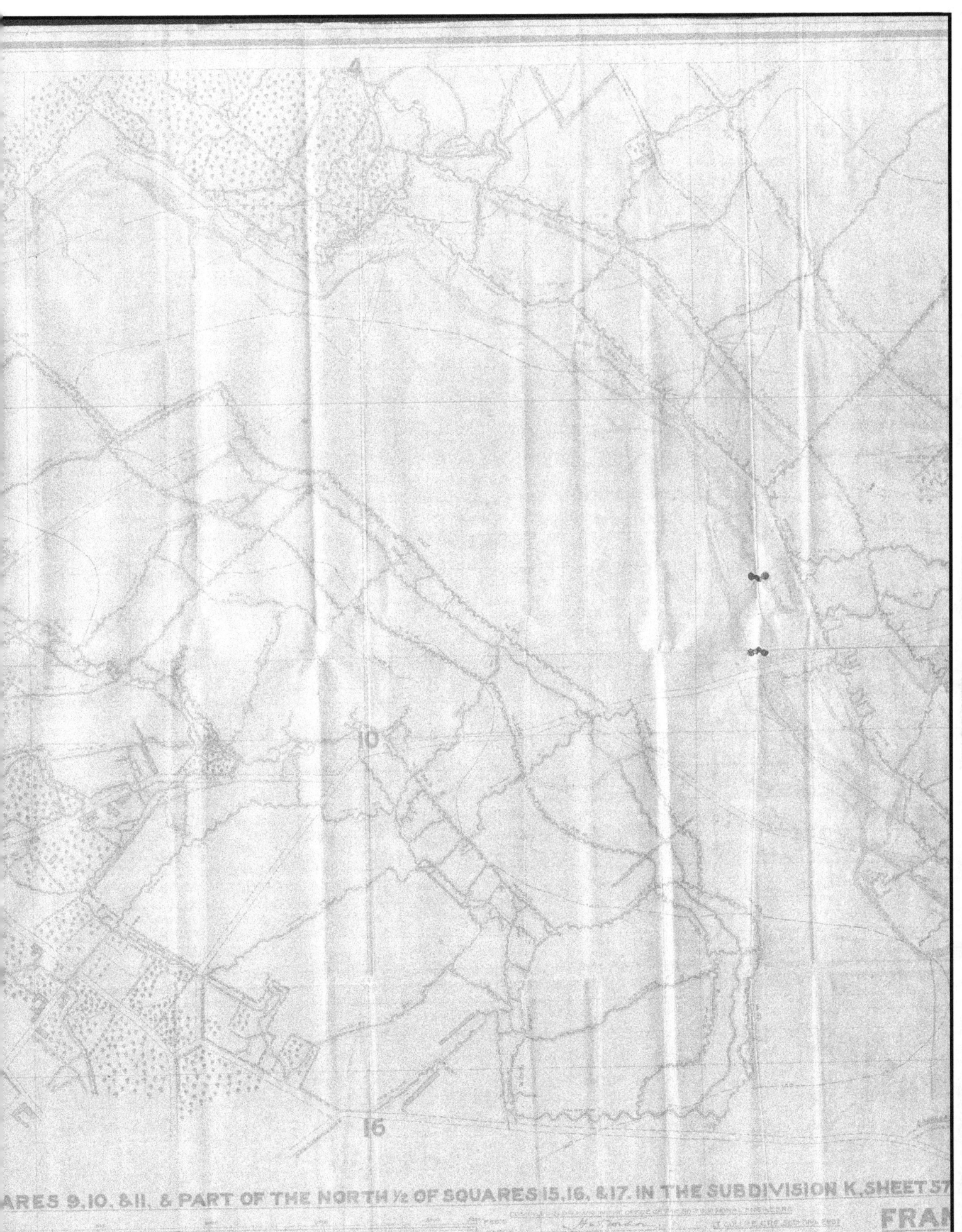

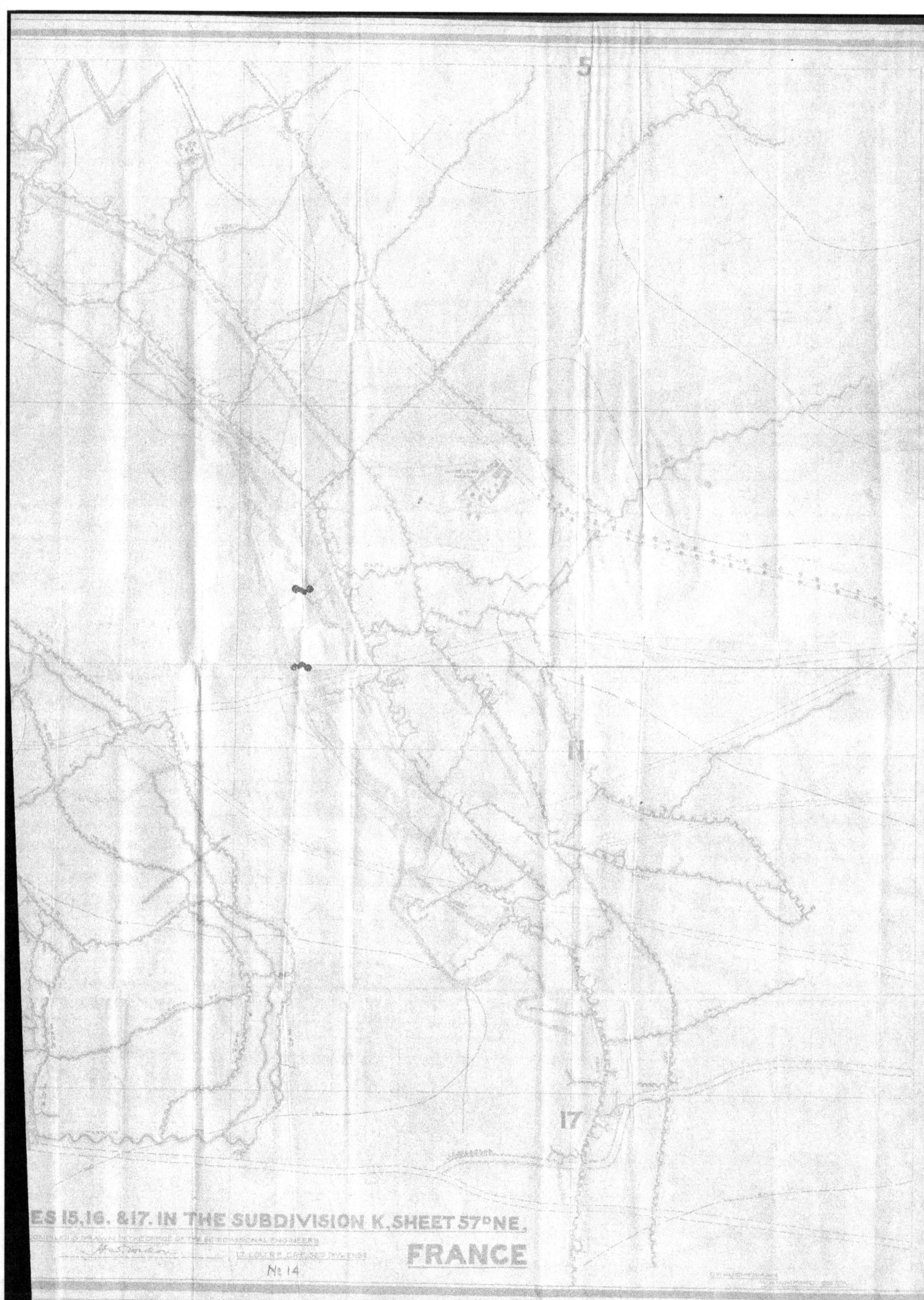

Appdx 2

Appendix C

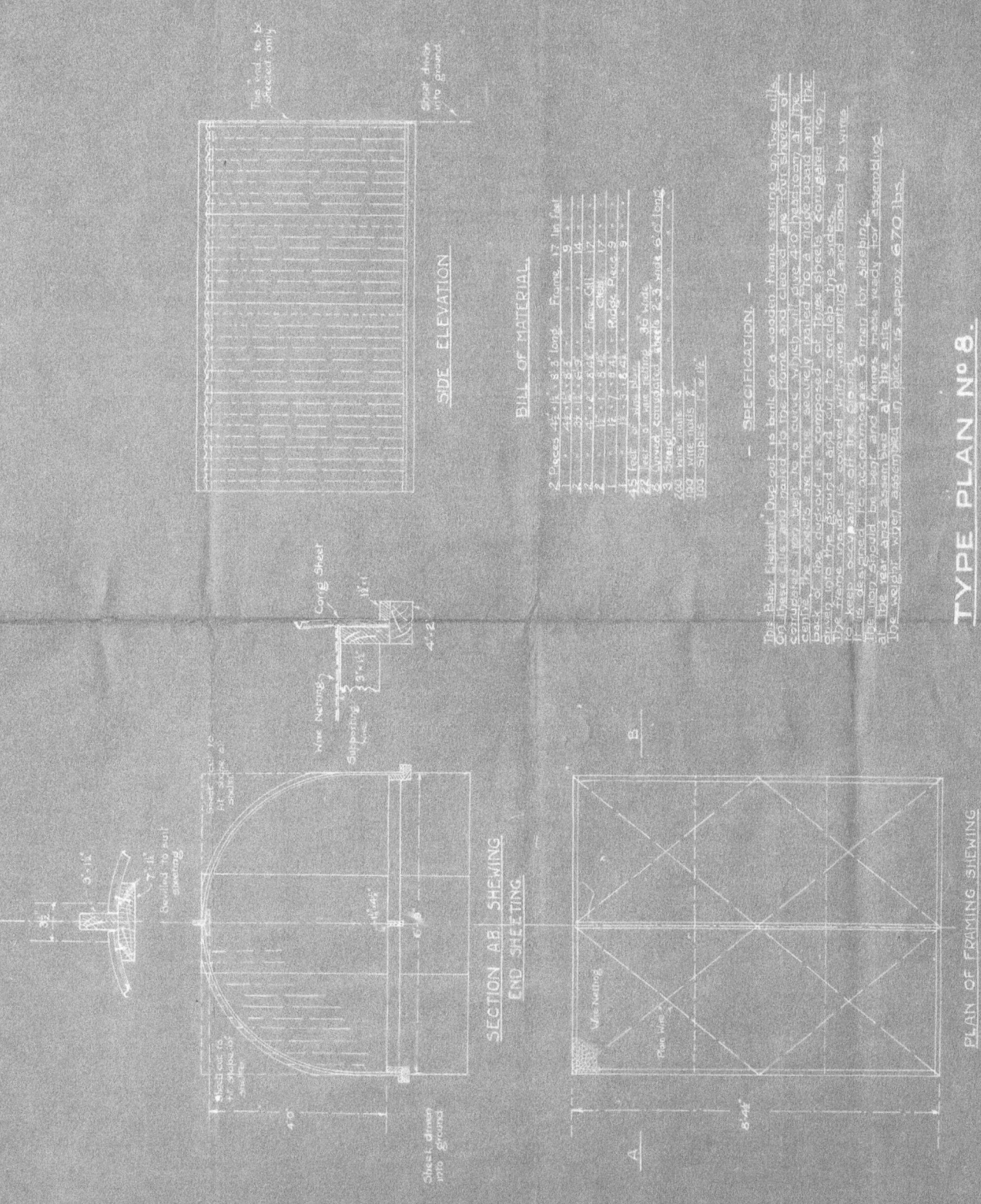

Appendix D.

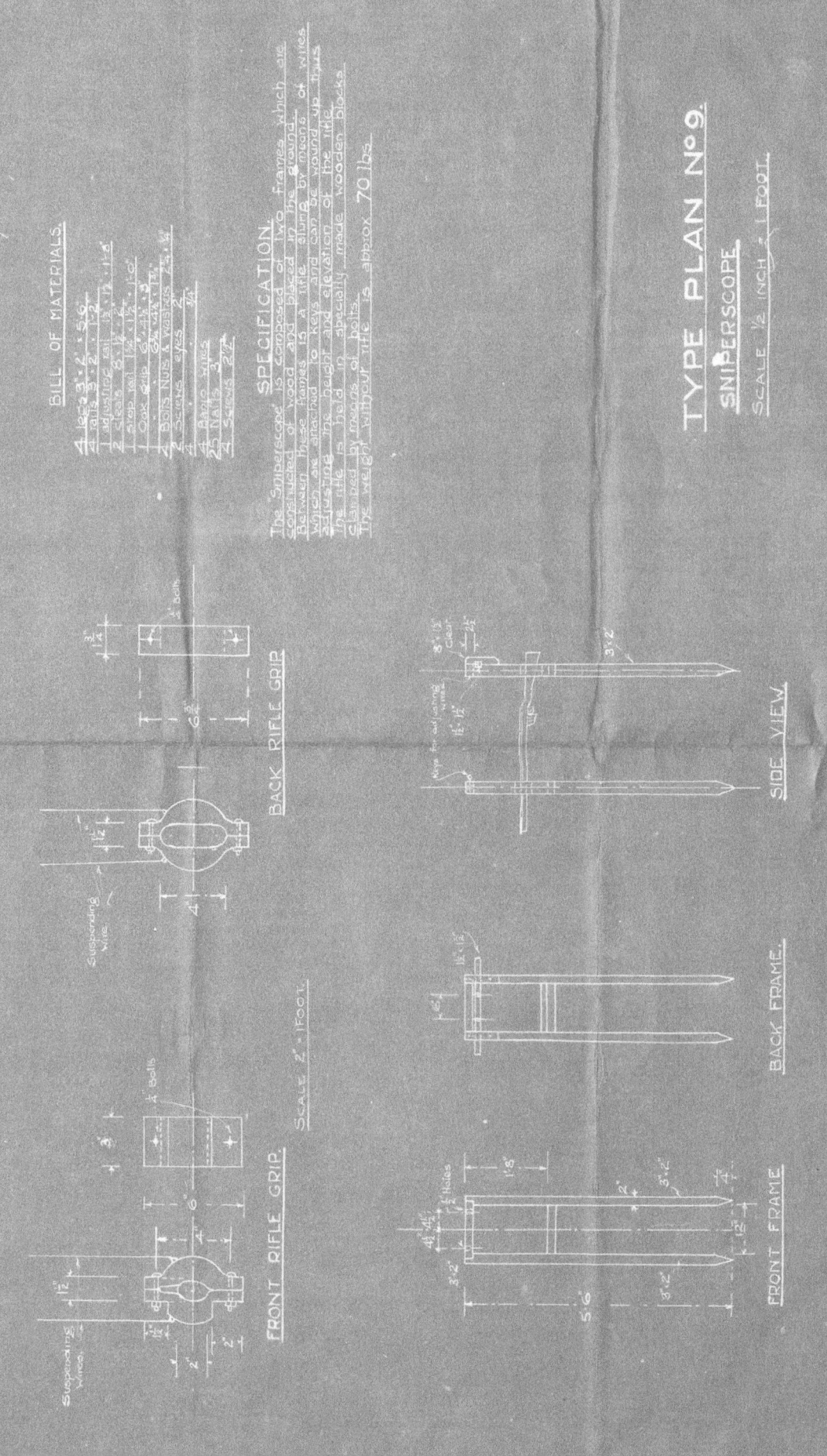

O/C Party 1st London Regiment.   SECRET.
"   " 3rd   "   "

Apdx 3

Reference proposed work on Communication Trenches, I attach a copy of map showing the position of same.

On the night of 19th inst it is proposed to dig forward 100 yards on the two centre communication trenches, i.e. from WOOD STREET towards junction of FETTER and ELBE and from YELLOW STREET towards salient corner in FERRET.   75 men will be used on each of these trenches.   Also to dig 50 yards forward on trench from corner of "Z" hedge to corner of GOMMECOURT PARK and 50 yards forward on trench from W.48 towards sap from FARM YARD.   30 men will be employed on each of these latter.

Gaps in our wire will be previously cut if necessary and steps made out of front line.   The general direction of the trenches will be previously marked, by Hambro lines.

The parties will parade and collect tools and sandbags at the Keep HEBUTERNE as regards the left party and at the 2/2nd Field Co. R.E. Store as regards the right party, at a time to be settled by Officers i/c working parties.

The trench to be dug should be 4' wide at the top, 2' wide at the bottom and 5' deep and diggers should be extended at 5' apart on right of Hamboro' line.

Capt. Smith 1/1 Edinburgh Field Co. R.E. will assist with the arrangements.   Covering parties for the above work will should be arranged by 167th Brigade.

Copy to H-Q, 167th Brigade.

Lieut. Col. R.E.
C.R.E., 56th Division.

17th June 1916.

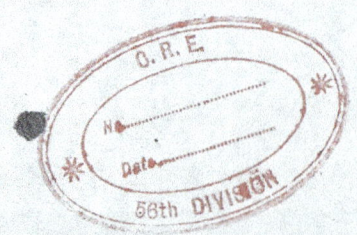

C.R/S 512.

(a) W.48 to FARMYARD Sap.   200 yds add 50 yds for staggers = 250 yds
(b) WOOD to ELBE   400 "   " 100 "   "   "   = 500 "
(c) YELLOW to FERRET   400 "   " 100 "   "   "   = 500 "
(d) "Z" hedge to FIR   266 "   " 64 "   "   "   = 330 =
                                          Total to be dug   1580

Night 22/23

(a) Dig 60 yds = 45 men ?)
(b) " 125 "   = 94   "   ) This allows 20% extra on 5' task
(c) " 125 "   = 94   "   )
(d) "   60 "   = 45   "   )

    Total   278   or 235 if (a) omitted.

"Z"

(a) Dig 190 yds = 143 men (or omit))
 or " 250 " = 188   "   )
)
(b) " 375 " = 282   "   ) Allows 20% extra on 5' task.
)
(c) " 375 " = 282   "   )
)
(d) " 270 " = 203   "   )

     Total (i) 955 if (a) dug completely on "Z" and no previous
                     work done on (a).
          (ii) 910 if (a) has been commenced on 22/23.
          (iii) 767 if (a) omitted altogether.

In case (I)   245 left for carrying forward stores
   " " (II) 290 "   "   "   "   "
   " " (III) 433 "   "   "   "   "

           If no work done 22/23 or any day before "Z"
                 Number of men required......1200

NOTES ON THE USE OF BANGALORE TORPEDOES

SECRET.

    The torpedoes are made up in 6' lengths and can be jointed together up to 4 lengths or 24'.

    Sappers are trained in the jointing, placing and fixing the torpedoes but should not be responsible for the selection of the portion of the enemy's wire to be destroyed.

    The torpedo will usually be employed to supplement the work of the Artillery in wire cutting. In most cases they will be placed at night at points selected on the previous day. The torpedo and its team (2 R.E.) and carrying party of 3) should be incorporated in a patrol, the patrol officer being in charge.

    The patrol will search the enemy's wire for the desired spot, the torpedo team and carrying party following behind. When the spot is found the patrol will lie down on either side and form a covering party and the torpedo will be placed in position. When all is ready a man will be sent back to report and the remainder will retire about 50 yards leaving one R.E. to light the fuse on a pre-arranged signal.

    Sufficient length of fuse will be used to enable the patrol to regain our trenches before the explosion.

Appdx 5

TYPE PLAN NO 10.
BANGALORE TORPEDO

LONGITUDINAL SECTION
Scale 1 inch = 1 foot

DETAIL OF JOINT AT "A".
Scale 3 inches = 1 foot

O/C,
1/1 City of Edinburgh Field Co.

Appendix 6

S.R/S 614 Copy No 4

SECRET.

The following is a list of the prospective work for your Company.

(1). Complete work in hand in order of urgency under orders of G.O.C., 167th Brigade.

(2). Ladders and bridges are to be in trenches before the relief of the 167th Brigade under supervision of Officers detailed by 168th and 169th Infantry Brigades. O/C Field Co. will assist.

(3) All ranks to be acquainted with the sites of all forward R.E. dumps 1 to 8.

(4) Immediately after the assault the O/C will be responsible for carrying forward dumps 2. 4. 6. and 8 to German line to dumps as under

2a in corner of FARM YARD K.11.c.6.8.

4a Junction of ELBE and FETTER.

6a Junction of EMDEN and FERN.

8a Junction of FIR and FEN.

168th and 169th Brigades will be responsible for carrying what they require from Nos. 1. 3. 5. and 7 dumps.

(5) During the last 65 minutes intensive bombardment on "Z" day the barriers on GOMMECOURT ROAD and BUCQUOY ROAD will be demolished, if necessary being prepared for small charges of explosive beforehand.

(6) Material must be collected beforehand in order to extend the wooden tramway down the GOMMECOURT ROAD.

(7) On "Z" day it will be necessary to run out a line showing direction for forward communication trenches i.e. from

(a) Sap between WHISKY and WELCOME STREET to Sap in FARM YARD

(b) WOOD STREET to ELBE.

(c) YELLOW STREET to Salient in FERRET.

(d) Corner of "Z" Hedge to junction of FIR and FIRM

The parties doing this will follow the assault immediately, and orders will be issued as to place of assembly of troops who will dig these C.T.s and the marking parties will be with their respective working parties.

As the advance will be made in smoke correct compass bearings must be taken beforehand.

Appendix 6

Major Samuel
Major Glover

Appx 7

1. Herewith a table showing the work to be done on forward communication trenches. As regards the trench (a) on list it has not yet been decided whether this trench will be dug or not. You will be informed as soon as a decision has been reached.

2. Arrangements will be made to have the portions marked out which are to be dug on night 22/23.

3. Both for purpose of dissimulation and for possible use, it would be well to form sap heads on night of 22/23.

4. On day "Z" it will probably be difficult to keep the alignment correctly. An endeavour will be made to peg out the line in advance as far as possible; failing this a compass bearing must be relied upon and it is suggested that a small party with a line on a reel go ahead on compass bearing to the objective paying out the line as they advance. The plan of trench to be aimed at is a zig-zag of about 8 or 9 paces each return.

Lieut. Col. R.E.
C.R.E., 56th Division.

19th June 1916.

Appendix 1

SECRET.

Appdx 8

C.R/S No. 15.
Copy No. 5.

1. The position of the R.E. Companies and Sections was given in table with my C.R/S 8. dated 24th June 1916.

2. O.C.s Companies should make arrangements so that any section is prepared to move off at a minutes notice on receipt of orders.

3. Special attention must be given to gas helmets and iron rations.

4. Attention of all O.C.s is drawn to pamphlet S.S. 108 "Notes on preparations for offensive operations" page 5 X "Tools carried on man by R.E." and provision made for equipping Sections. In case of emergency, tools from section carts may be used, but this should be avoided if possible, and if the tool carts have to be depleted, a report should be at once made to this Office.

5. The next few days should be devoted to training the Companies in consolidation of trenches, blocking trenches, and the use of the Bangalore Torpedo.

6. All reports to C.R.E. will be rendered to C.R.E's Office HENU till midday on "Y" day, after that to C.R.E. Advanced Divisional Headquarters, excepting routine reports which will be rendered as usual to C.R.E's Office HENU.

Reports from HEBUTERNE should be sent to Report Centre for transmission.

Lieut. Col. R.E.
C.R.E., 56th Division.

26th June 1916.

Appendix 8

Appendix A.

TYPE PLAN NO 6 A.
PORTABLE BRIDGE FOR FIELD ARTILLERY.
SCALE ½ INCH TO 1 FOOT.

SECTION A.B.

BILL OF MATERIAL

Decking	24 pieces 4x1½	5'-7" long
	3 " "	7'-0"
	1 " 5x2	7'-6"
	2 " 3x1½	2'-3"
	2 " log 3	2'-6"
Traisons	2 " 2x1½	7'-3"
	2 " 2x1½	3'-0"
Beams	2 " 4x3	13'-0"
	2 " 4x3	8'-0"
	1 " 4x1½	4'-3"
	2 " 5x2	13'-0"
	2 " 4x1½	2'-6"
	2 " 4x1½	2'-9"
	2 Iron Straps 2¼x¼	
	6 Bolts, T washers	
	2 Iron Pins ⅜x8"	
	4 Rope Handles	
	300 Wire Nails	3"

SPECIFICATION

The bridge is constructed to take field Artillery over trenches without upsetting teams. It can be carried on a gun limber and is portable. It is composed of three separate beams (wings) as supported at each end by a cross piece of wood (sill). The beams are composed of three 2"x3" connected by cleats on a horizontal plane of three 2" x 3" pieces separate pieces compose a deck, and rest on the cleats, falling into a groove in the beam and sliding its place. The long end of the beam acting as a support when the bridge is thrown across a trench. An iron strap of iron bolted to the beam and pinned to the girders on either side by a bolt pin.

PLAN DECK REMOVED

PLAN DECK IN PLACE

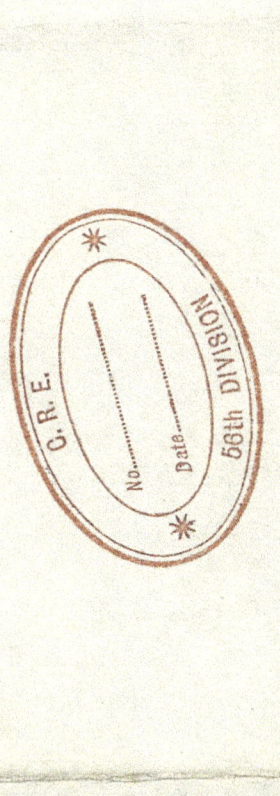

Appendix B

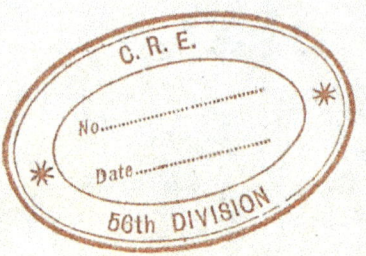

BILL OF MATERIAL

slats	30 pieces	1¾ x ½	1'6" long	45 lin feet
ribs	2	2 x 1	10'0"	20 " "
pieces	2	1¼ x ½	10'0"	20 " "
struts	6	¼ x ½	1'0"	6 " "
stiffeners	6	2½ x 1	1'0"	6 " "
nails	100		1 wire	
screws	2 doz			
hoop iron	40 lin feet	½ x 1/16		
handles	2 pieces	1¼ x 2'6" long		5 lin feet

SPECIFICATION

This portable bridge is constructed of very light material and consequently must be very firmly put together.
The bridge consists of two beams with a decking of slats. These slats are supported in the center by a rib fixed at each end to the handles.
Each beam consists of a rib as compression member and a band of hoop iron as tension member, these are forced apart by three struts thus forming the camber to the bridge.
The ribs are morticed into the struts and the center struts are lightly braced.
The total weight of the bridge is 28 lbs.

TYPE PLAN N°4
PORTABLE BRIDGE
SCALE ½ INCH = 1 FOOT

PLAN

SECTIONAL ELEVATION

SECTION THROUGH CENTER

56th Division.

C. R. E.

56th DIVISIONAL ENGINEERS.

J U L Y

1916

Attached:

Reports on the Operations
1.7.16 by

C.R.E.
2/1st Lond.Field Coy.) Sec-
2/2nd :   :   :) tions.

SECRET.

Army Form C. 2118.

Instructions regarding War Diaries and Intelligence Summaries are contained in F.S. Regs., Part II. and the Staff Manual respectively. Title pages will be prepared in manuscript.

WAR DIARY
or
INTELLIGENCE SUMMARY.
(Erase heading not required.)

Headquarters 58th Divn. R.E.

Vol 6

Place	Date	Hour	Summary of Events and Information	Remarks and references to Appendices
HENU	1.7.16		C.R.E. at Advr. Divn. H.Q. SOUASTRE. Adjutant at Office HENU. Attack on Enemy lines in progress. BANGALORE Torpedoes used at night.	
"	2.7.16	2pm	C.R.E. returned from SOUASTRE.	
"	3.7.16		Received Reports of Operations from Lt. J.E. Villa 2/2 Lond Fd. Co & Lt. H.A. Scott 2/1 Lond. Fd. Co. - Instructions received to take over FONQUEVILLERS Section of the line in addition to area already held - Took over 46th Divisional Dump at PAS. - Arranged Dumps for the 2/3 Field Coys. & worked out methods of dealing with stores & labour. Instructions issued for Officer of 132nd A.T. Coy to visit Gun positions to ascertain requirements of the Artillery.	
"	4.7.16		C.R.E. walked Front Line HEBUTERNE - found front line badly cramped up by reason of enemy bombardment of night 2/3. also visited FONQUEVILLERS - & made note of work required in both places. - Received large bundle of papers from C.R.E. 46th Divn. - went through same & extracted formulas of work in progress in FONQUEVILLERS - Went into question of re organisation of	

Army Form C. 2118

WAR DIARY
or
INTELLIGENCE SUMMARY.

(Erase heading not required.)

Instructions regarding War Diaries and Intelligence Summaries are contained in F. S. Regs., Part II. and the Staff Manual respectively. Title pages will be prepared in manuscript.

Place	Date	Hour	Summary of Events and Information	Remarks and references to Appendices
HENU	4/7/16		Method of working the Field Companies & drew out plan allotting sub-area to each Company so as to ensure continuity of work. Received allotment of Artillery Timber for July from C.E. 7th Corps.	
"	5/7/16		C.E. 7th Corps called & discussed the various questions arising on taking over the FONQUEVILLERS Area. — C.R.E. worked area with him. Made up estimate of R.E. materials required for August for 6 & 7th Corps. Instructions to Edinburgh Fd Co to survey & report on existing DECAUVILLE track & possibilities of its extension.	
"	6/7/16		Prepared & issued circular & plan allotting out the areas allotted to the 3 Field Cos. — Instructions issued to 2/2nd Field Co to proceed with erection of baths at SOUASTRE & 5th AMMND to consult respective Town Majors to fix sites etc.	
"	7/7/16		Received information that 152nd & 153rd Field Coys would be coming into area to work — considering question of their employment & settling as to work to be done by each Company — Interview with Staff Capt 168th Brigade in regard to the allotment of Field Coys	

WAR DIARY
or
INTELLIGENCE SUMMARY.
(Erase heading not required.)

Army Form C. 2118

Instructions regarding War Diaries and Intelligence Summaries are contained in F. S. Regs., Part II. and the Staff Manual respectively. Title pages will be prepared in manuscript.

Place	Date	Hour	Summary of Events and Information	Remarks and references to Appendices
HENU	7.7.16		& explaining how this would affect him. Issued orders in regard to disposition & movement of 152nd & 153rd Field Coys. Received recommendations for honours from the 3 Field Coys. in regard to the 1st July operations. Received report from the Signal Coy. Received report from Edinburgh Field C on Decauville Track & intended for material required to complete track.	
	8.7.16		C.R.E. visited COIGNEUX district to settle location for Field C. dumps & site for baths. Received O.O.IV.19. Interviewed officers Commandg. of 152nd & 153rd Field Coys & explained works in progress & methods of working. Saw the Edinburgh Field C & discussed questions of water supply HEBUTERNE & issued instructions as to work to be done	
	9.7.16 9am		152nd & 153rd Field Companies formed Division temporarily C.R.E. visited trenches. inspected works in progress & took note of various small matters for discussion with Officer C. Companies C.R.E. visited PAS. Interviewed C.E. & informed him of what	

WAR DIARY
or
INTELLIGENCE SUMMARY.
(Erase heading not required.)

Place	Date	Hour	Summary of Events and Information	Remarks and references to Appendices
HENU	9.7.16		was being done -	
	10.7.16		Received report from 2/1st Field C.E. report to HEBUTERNE Water Supply. Consolidary sketch of BAYENCOURT Bath received from 2/1st Edinburgh Field C.E. - same forwarded to C.E. 1st Corps. Consolidary suggestions for shell proof shelters for No 1 Well HEBUTERNE Order issued to Edinburgh Field C.E. to send two sections to HEBUTERNE	
	11.7.16		C.R.E. visited site selected for Bathhouse with A.D.M.S discussing with him the plans suggested for drainage & water supply - 153rd Field Company came under orders of 3/rd Division - Arrangements made for removal of 2/1 Field C.E. dump - Report on use of horses dishoysen sent to C.E VIIth Corps at his request -	
	12.7.16		C.R.E. visited HEBUTERNE & FONQUEVILLERS with Brigade Major 167 Brigade going round trenches in his sector with him & orthoning works which were considered urgently necessary 1st C.T.s 2nd trenches 3rd dugouts & discussing these matters with him & question of labour Instructions issued to Edinburgh Fd. C.E. to proceed with BAYENCOURT Bathhouse	

Army Form C. 2118.

WAR DIARY
or
INTELLIGENCE SUMMARY.
(Erase heading not required.)

Instructions regarding War Diaries and Intelligence Summaries are contained in F.S. Regs., Part II. and the Staff Manual respectively. Title pages will be prepared in manuscript.

Place	Date	Hour	Summary of Events and Information	Remarks and references to Appendices
HENU	13.7.16		162nd Field Co left Duncan – 2/1 Field Co instructed to take over stores left behind by them.	
	14.7.16		C.R.E. visited front line trenches	
	15.7.16		Intimation received that 169 Brigade would require Bangalore Torpedoes – construction of same put in hand – Went into question of protected cable SAILLY- The G.O.C. 168th Brigade having asked for dugouts for 400 men. Interview with G.O.C. 168 Brigade in regard to his requirements + arranging to strengthen protect cellar accommodation already in existence. Arrangements made by D.H.Q. for use of Chaux Park Majors for carting R.E. stores	
	16.7.16		Conference with O.s. C. Companies in regard to their responsibilities now that the Divisional area had been subdivided + setting out lines to be adopted in regard to R.E. work.	
	17.7.16		C.R.E. visited FONQUEVILLERS & BIENVILLERS inspecting of works in progress. Adjutant visited HEBUTERNE + inspected works in progress there. Received intimation that as gunpowder	

WAR DIARY or INTELLIGENCE SUMMARY

Army Form C. 2118.

Instructions regarding War Diaries and Intelligence Summaries are contained in F.S. Regs., Part II. and the Staff Manual respectively. Title pages will be prepared in manuscript.

(Erase heading not required.)

Place	Date	Hour	Summary of Events and Information	Remarks and references to Appendices
HENU	17/7/16		Corps would take over responsibility for roads. Divisions would work under the C.R.E. on immediate necessary work. Information received as to boundaries of 5th Div: Area.	
	18/7/16		Received orders that rooms used as offices must be vacated as quickly as possible as they were required by Commander-Corps H.A. C.R.E. visited trenches to note progress of work by Companies.	
	19/7/16		Offices moved. Telephone installed within 1 hour of arrival.	
	20/7/16		C.R.E. & Adjutant visited HEBUTERNE & FONQUEVILLERS - inspected work done & in progress. Instructed Edinburgh Fd. Co to carry out re-arrangement of horse troughs BAYENCOURT.	
	21/7/16		C.R.E. attended conference at Adv: Div: HQ. - Instructions issued to Edinburgh Fd. Co to make mine cases - also to demolish concrete posts on roads. Orders issued to 2/1 Field Co that work on Whiskey & Warrior Sheds must be carried on speedily.	
	22/7/16		Inspection of TAS hutments - making notes of works required	

WAR DIARY
or
INTELLIGENCE SUMMARY.

(Erase heading not required.)

Army Form C. 2118.

Instructions regarding War Diaries and Intelligence Summaries are contained in F.S. Regs., Part II. and the Staff Manual respectively. Title pages will be prepared in manuscript.

Place	Date	Hour	Summary of Events and Information	Remarks and references to Appendices
HENU	22.7.16		C.R.E visited front line trenches.	
	24.7.16		Ditto - C.E supplied with sketch plan of Bayencourt Light Railway.	
	25.7.16		C.R.E. visited C.R.E. 38th Division - Adjutant went to HEBUTERNE & also visited Dumps of 2/1st and inspected works in progress there & 2/2nd Co Companies.	
	26.7.16		Machinery Distribution Return prepared for C.E. 7th Corps - C.R.E. visited Edinburgh Sector of line north of Co Company -	
	27.7.16		C.R.E accompanied C.E. 3rd Army on inspection of trenches -	
	28.7.16		Officers C. Companies instructed to prepare scheme of work proposed in time for conference on Sunday.	
	29.7.16		Conversing question of water supplies for FONQUEVILLERS & Chateau de la Haie.	
	30.7.16		Consultation with O.s. C. Id Companies discussing the progress of work in their respective sectors & informing them of what was expected from each Company in regard to reconstruction work	

WAR DIARY
or
INTELLIGENCE SUMMARY.
(Erase heading not required.)

Army Form C. 2118.

Instructions regarding War Diaries and Intelligence Summaries are contained in F.S. Regs., Part II. and the Staff Manual respectively. Title pages will be prepared in manuscript.

Place	Date	Hour	Summary of Events and Information	Remarks and references to Appendices
HENU	30/7/16		Inspection by C.E. 4th Corps of roads in forward area - C.R.E. visited trenches - Adjutant engaged inspecting officers & men	
	31/7/16		from 167 Brigade in construction of demolitions by Bangalore Torpedoes. Issued notes to Field Companies for their consideration on work to be done in case of an advance	
			Generally the month proved an exceedingly busy one owing to the large amount of restoration required in the front line and C.T.s. The work & difficulties were largely increased owing to the excessive rains in the early part of the month.	

2nd August 1916

[signature]
for Lt Col [?] R.E.
C.R.E. 57th Division
Capt

SECRET.

G.O.C.	
G.S.O. 1	
G.S.O. 2	
G.S.O. 3	

C.R/S. 51.

3. C.

Headquarters,
56th Division.

From what has been reported by the R.E. Officers who accompanied the attacking troops in the recent operations, the following points seem to be worthy of notice.

1. The success or failure of an attack with even the best troops depends on the communications. Once the first elan of the attack was expended the enemy snipers and artillery dominated "No man's land" and it was impossible to get forward supplies of bombs and ammunition. Although the parties of the attacking force to which they were attached suffered from Artillery fire, in both cases they were eventually bombed out of their positions.

Both Officers are confident that had it not been for lack of bombs and ammunition the parties could have held their own until nightfall.

In any future operations of a similar nature it would seem worth while taking a big risk, in order to get communications dug the night before the attack.

2. It is questionable whether it is advisable to send a large number of R.E. over with the attack. If the attack is successful R.E. can be sent over later to help to consolidate the captured positions, whereas if the attack is unsuccessful the R.E. are unable to do any good at their own work and merely get involved in work for which they are not trained.

On the other hand it would appear desirable to detail parties composed of Infantry and R.E. armed with 10lb and smaller charges of explosives to clear up trenches and destroy dug-outs, trench mortars, M.G. emplacements etc.

In the late operation a M.G. which was captured was not destroyed and was very probably one of those subsequently

(2)

used against us from GOMMECOURT PARK.

In the strong point at FARMYARD there were about 11 Minnenwerfer ~~some~~ none of which seem to have been destroyed, this is explained by the fact that the R.E. had their special work to carry out in blocking the trenches and when this was finished they were involved in repelling the counter attacks of the enemy.

5.   The German bombers appear to have used Very lights in order to show their own position and also to direct the fire of their supporting Artillery.   The falling of a Very light in the trenches taken by us was followed by shrapnel on the part indicated.

[signature]
Lieut, Col, R.E.
C.R.E., 56th Division.

7th July 1916.

CONFIDENTIAL.

8.B.

C.R.E.,
    56th Division.

    With reference to your C.R.S./39 of the 3rd instant - there is at present no definite information available that our troops ever reached the Quadrilateral. Perhaps 2nd Lieut. SCOTT can provide the evidence, as from his report he seems confident that one of his parties was working there.

Hdqrs. 56th Divn.
4th July, 1916.

                              Lieut. Colonel,
                              General Staff.

Confidential

Headquarters,
56th Division

I beg to forward herewith copies of Reports received from the Officers of the Sections of the 2/1st and 2/2nd London Field Companies detailed to accompany the Infantry in the assault during the recent operations.

Lieut. Col. R.E.
C.R.E., 56th Division.

3rd July 1916.

2/2nd London Field Co.
2.7.16

From,
　Lieut. J.E.Villa R.E.
　　O. i/c No. 1 Section
　　　2/2nd London Field Co.

To,
　C.R.E.,
　　56th Division.

　　　　I have the honour to submit a report on the work done by my section in the recent operations.

　　　　The section was attached to the London Scottish for orders and with the approval of the C.O. London Scottish was divided up into 4 blocking parties, each consisting of a Junior N.C.O. and 4 Sappers (with a Senior N.C.O. in charge of each pair of parties); and a Reserve of 10 men under the Section Sergeant. The Blocking Parties were attached to respective companies and the Reserve to Battalion Headquarters. Their work consisted of ;-
Firstly The blocking of the trenches FAIR, FANCY, FACT, and FABLE leading to strong point at K.11,c.6.8.
Secondly Consolidation of strong point.

　　　　With reference to the blocking parties of Sappers working in conjunction with the working parties of the London Scottish two blocks were made in Trench FAIR with the aid of explosives, a loop-hole for Lewis-gunner was constructed and wire entanglement placed in front of the block. This was held very successfully until the arrival of German reinforcements forced the men into the strong point.

　　　　In FANCY no explosives were used owing to the conditinn of the trench which was practically filled in.

　　　　In FACT two traverses were blown in with the aid of explosives but the bombing party in advance of the working party was forced back causing the men to withdraw to the strong point making a hasty barrier in front of them. This was held for a considerable period by rifle fire both sappers and infantry working together in manning the trenches.

(2)

In FABLE all the sappers were killed or severely wounded owing to the trench not being cleared, but this could not be done owing to the constant stream of German reserves that were coming along FAME via FELON and ELBE.

The remainder of the parties and those working in the strong point itself were gathered under the command of Major Lindsay of the London Scottish and a determined stand made to hold the strong point, but the withdrawal of our left flank made the situation very critical, resulting in a withdrawal to our own lines under very heavy shell fire.

In conclusion I wish to mention that the Infantry and Engineers worked so completely in unison with one another that I cannot help but expressing the admiration and respect No. 1 Section has for the Officers and men of the London Scottish with whom it has been our good fortune to work.

I have the honour to be,

Sir,

Yours obediently,

(Sd) J.E.Villa

Lieut. R. E.

HENU

2. 7. 16.

From,
   2nd Lieut. H.A.Scott R.E.
      Officer i/c No. 1 Section
         2/1st London Field Co.

To,
   C.R.E.,
      56th Division.

        I have the honour to submit a report of the work done by my Section in the recent operations.

        The distribution of my Section was as follows:-

        6 Sappers 1 N.C.O.   L.R.B.

        6 Sappers 1 N.C.O.   Q.V.R.

        14 Sappers 1 N.C.O.   Q.W.R.

and the work allotted to them was **Firstly** the blocking of Communication Trenches and **Secondly** Consolidation of Strong Points which were five in number

These were :-
1. GOMMECOURT Strong Point
2. THE MAZE " "
3. THE CEMETERY " "
4. THE QUADRILATERAL Strong Point.
5. THE INDUS " "

    With reference to the first of these GOMMECOURT one communication trench was blocked, a Bombing Post constructed and work begun on reversing trenches but this had to be abandoned owing to an attack by German bombers.

    A supply of 400 German bombs was discovered in the vicinity which was promptly used by the party against the enemy.

2.   **The MAZE Strong Point.**   The communication trenches were blocked and wired, short lengths of Fire trenches were dug and trenches reversed, but on being attacked both Infantry and Engineers were compelled to abandon work and man the trenches

3. In the CEMETERY Strong Point I have little or no confirmation of any useful R.E. work being done owing to all the Sappers in the party being missing.

4. QUADRILATERAL Strong Point. The work carried on here was more or less in consolidating the position gained by building a barricade and firing step and blowing in traverses with the aid of explosives.

5. INDUS Strong Point. No reports about this position have reached me owing to the Sappers attached to this party being missing.

I should like to mention in conclusion the splendid behaviour of the Sappers and that there was always a mutual co-operation between the Infantry and R.E. which helped the work on considerably.

I have the honour to be,

Sir,

Yours obediently,

(Sd) H. A. Scott

2nd Lieut. R.E.

HENU

3/7/16.

56th Divisional Engineers

C. R. E.

56th DIVISION.

AUGUST 1 9 1 6

WAR DIARY
or
INTELLIGENCE SUMMARY.

(Erase heading not required.)

Army Form C. 2118

Instructions regarding War Diaries and Intelligence Summaries are contained in F.S. Regs., Part II. and the Staff Manual respectively. Title pages will be prepared in manuscript.

Place	Date	Hour	Summary of Events and Information	Remarks and references to Appendices
HENU	1.8.16		Instructions received that arrangements for installing gas were to be put in hand at once. Interview with O.C. 4th Batt". Special Brigade R.E. discussed matter fully with him & setting out arrangements proposed in order to meet his requirements. Got out features of scheme & "Preges". Prepared table of working parties required.	
"	2.8.16		Submitted to D.H.Q. scheme of work proposed for Companies. Adjutant visited FONQUEVILLERS with the 4th Batt". Special Brigade arranging as to special fire steps - work organised - work on Russian saps organised. Table showing working parties required to Companies. (C.R.E. S/1.53)	
"	3.8.16		Interview with Inspector of Mines. Informed him of proposed work. C.R.E. worked therefore with G.S.O.2 to reconnoitre in connection with special fire steps.	
"	4.8.16		Interview with O's.C. 2/1st & Edinburgh L. Coys respecting reports on special work in hand discussing same with them. C.R.E. & Adjutant visited Lacks area & Divisional School. Received orders that special detachments were to be housed in rapid succession - getting out instructions to	

WAR DIARY
or
INTELLIGENCE SUMMARY.

(Erase heading not required.)

Army Form C. 2118

Place	Date	Hour	Summary of Events and Information	Remarks and references to Appendices
HENU	4.8.16		particulars for use in connection therewith.	
"	5.8.16		C.R.E. & Adjutant visited FONQUEVILLERS inspected special work in progress part of area reconnoitred for chalk. Dump at PAS closed.	
"	6.8.16		C.R.E. visited trenches with G.S.O.3 inspected work in progress on special fire steps - winter accesses - mined dug outs etc.	
"	7.8.16		C.R.E. visited AMIENS purchasing stores. Adjutant visited C.R.E. 46th Divn. Experiments carried out with barbed wire concertina entanglements.	
"	8.8.16	7am	Received D.O. No 21 setting out arrangements made for installing gas on front in places selected. C.R.E. visited trenches in Right Brigade Sector inspected work in progress there. Adjutant visited MONDICOURT in reference to stores	
"	9.8.16		C.R.E. visited HEBUTERNE + FONQUEVILLERS inspected works in progress there	
"	10.8.16	2.30pm	Received D.O. No 22 as to installation of gas cylinders.	
"	11.8.16		C.R.E. visited trenches in FONQUEVILLERS area	
"	12.8.16		Nil	
"	13.8.16		C.R.E. visited PAS conferred with Chief Engineer	

Army Form C. 2118.

WAR DIARY
or
INTELLIGENCE SUMMARY.
(Erase heading not required.)

Instructions regarding War Diaries and Intelligence Summaries are contained in F.S. Regs., Part II. and the Staff Manual respectively. Title pages will be prepared in manuscript.

C.R.E.
50th DIVISION

Place	Date	Hour	Summary of Events and Information	Remarks and references to Appendices
HENU	12.8.16	6.5pm	Received orders in regard to repair of dug-outs CALVAIRE Trod Inspection of Horses & Vehicles of the three Companies by C.R.E. and Adjutant	
"	14.8.16		Received D.O. N° 23 notifying arrangements for gas discharge. " " N° 24 warning that Division was about to be relieved. C.R.E. visited trenches with G.E. & VII Corps. Received orders from DHQ as to form in which handing over statements should be prepared & of the information required to be given. Revising work programme submitted at beginning of month accordingly & instructions issued to Companies to submit revised schedule.	
"	15.8.16		C.R.E. visited proposed hunting area with Staff.	
"	16.8.16		Adjutant visited LUCHEUX completed arrangements for watering horses there of 50 Div en route to new area. Arrangements completed for stores & horse lines to be available immediately on arrival. Received D.O. 25 giving detailed programme for relief. Orders issued to Field Companies & drivers on rly end to ensure. Received instruction for billeting whilst on way.	

Army Form C. 2118.

WAR DIARY
or
INTELLIGENCE SUMMARY.
(Erase heading not required.)

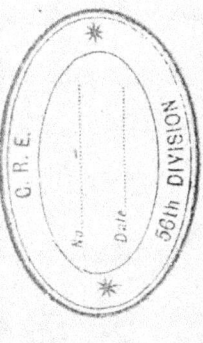
C.R.E.
56th DIVISION

Instructions regarding War Diaries and Intelligence Summaries are contained in F.S. Regs., Part II. and the Staff Manual respectively. Title pages will be prepared in manuscript.

Place	Date	Hour	Summary of Events and Information	Remarks and references to Appendices
HENU	17.8.16		C.R.E. 17th Divsn called - showed + explained to him the works in progress - and C.R.E. noted front of trenches with him -	
"	18.8.16		C.R.E. visited front line trenches with C.R.E. 17th Divn & continued hand-over. Instructions issued to Companies in regard to billetting arrangements whilst on move. Orders issued to Field Companies to leave one officer behind for two or three days to assist relieving Field Companies in taking over - Letter to Companies asking for programme of work proposed whilst on hauling over -	
"	19.8.16		Drew up + circulated instructions for having so as to ensure uniformity of ideas + lines to be adopted.	
"	20.8.16		Received D.O. 27 giving alteration in moves - Orders issued to Field Coys in accordance therewith - Handed over to C.R.E. 17th Divsn all papers, instructions, sketches etc referring to work in Divisional Area - + handed over stores -	
DOULLENS	21.8.16		H.Q. moved to DOULLENS arrived 1-30 p.m.	
FROHEN	22.8.16		March continued - arrived FROHEN-LE-GRAND - 2-30 p.m.	
ST RIQUIER	23.8.16		Ditto arrived ST RIQUIER 4 p.m.	

WAR DIARY or INTELLIGENCE SUMMARY.

Army Form C. 2118.

(Erase heading not required.)

Instructions regarding War Diaries and Intelligence Summaries are contained in F. S. Regs., Part II. and the Staff Manual respectively. Title pages will be prepared in manuscript.

C.R.E.
No. 60/334
Date 2/9/16
50th DIVISION

Place	Date	Hour	Summary of Events and Information	Remarks and references to Appendices
ST. RIQUIER	24.8.16		C.R.E. visited training ground & the 3 Companies & discussed various points in regard to training with O's. C.	
"	25.8.16		Training of Companies commenced. C.R.E. visited Companies & made notes of points for further consideration.	
"	26.8.16		Conference with O's. C. Companies discussing training in progress & pointing out various defects which I wished remedied. C.R.E. visited Companies on practice on night wiring.	
"	27. "		Training continued	
"	28. "		do	
"	29. "		do	
"	30. "		do	
"	31. "		do	

Jas Forlin
Lt Col R.E.
C.R.E. 50th Div.

56th Divisional Engineers

C. R. E.

56th DIVISION.

SEPTEMBER 1916.

Appendices :- Notes on Training.
Report on Work of R.E. & Pioneers.

Army Form C.2118

WAR DIARY or INTELLIGENCE SUMMARY

(Erase heading not required.)

H.Q. 56th Divn R.E.

Place	Date	Hour	Summary of Events and Information	Remarks and references to Appendices
ST RIQUIER	1.9.16		Received D.O. No 28 ordering move - Training of R.E. and Infantry concluded.	Appendix A
"	2.9.16		Memo of lines adopted attached. Preparing for move - Received D.O. No 29 -	
"	3.9.16		Transport & mounted detachment left for new area by road	
"	4.9.16		Remainder moved to CORBIE by train - Arrived 1-30 p.m. -	
CORBIE	5.9.16		Received D.O. No 30 -	
"	6.9.16		Moved to FORKED TREE -	
FORKED TREE	7.9.16		" H.Q. at BILLON FARM.	
BILLON FARM	8.9.16		Reconnaissance of forward area by C.R.E. and visited C.R.E. 5th Division	
"	9.9.16		Work organised & Companies well commenced.	
"	10.9.16		Received D.O. No 34	
"	11.9.16			
"	12.9.16		Received D.O. No 35, 36 & 37 -	
"	13.9.16		Special conference with O.s.C. Companies	
"	14.9.16		Received D.O. No 38 & Warning Order regarding operations.	

Army Form C.2118

WAR DIARY
or
INTELLIGENCE SUMMARY

(Erase heading not required.)

H.Q.
56 Div¹. R.E

Place	Date	Hour	Summary of Events and Information	Remarks and references to Appendices
BILLON FARM	15.9.16		—	
	16.9.16		C.R.E. Hq⁶. & E.C. Sergt. moved to BATTLE H.Q. (A.10.b.5.5)	
BATTLE HQ	17.9.16		Received O.O. 40.	
"	18.9.16		" " 41	
"	20.9.16		" " 42	
BILLON FARM	21.9.16		Returned to Div¹ H.Q. at BILLON FARM.	
"	22.9.16		A/C.S.M. Paine L. joined from 226th Coy. as A/R.S.M.	
"	23.9.16		Received O.O. 43.	
"	24.9.16		" Appendices A & B to above O.O.	
"	25.9.16		Received O.O 44.	
"	26.9.16		—	
"	27.9.16		Received O.O. 95 & 96.	
"	28.9.16		" " 47.	
"	29.9.16		" " 48	
"	30.9.16		" " 49	
"			" " 50	
			Copy Report of work of R.E and Pioneers as attached - - - -	Appx B

[signature]
Lt. Colt.
C.R.E. 56th Div.
3/10/16

Appdx A

NOTES ON TRAINING OF R.E. COMPANY and ATTACHED

The training should be carried out at top pressure and should be made as interesting as possible.

It is suggested that the actual working hours should be not more than 6 hours per day excluding lectures, physical training etc.

The training must be designed for everyone, Officers, N.C.O's as well as men, every occasion for instruction should be made full use of.

All officers and senior N.C.O. should submit daily to O.C. Company a report on the days work - these to be discussed at a nightly conference. These reports are extremely important during operations.

The training should consist of the following:-

COMPANY DRILL. To be carried out in three periods of one hour each - smartness and quickness being the important factors. Officers should take their sections separately as well.

B. HANDLING and DETAILING working parties without tracing. TRAINING men to get on to their work and spitlock their tasks quickly and quietly.

A good method of tracing a trench and detailing men is as follows The party is led to the beginning of the work in Indian file at about two paces interval by the Officer or N.C.O. responsible for the siting of the trench, who has if possible reconnoitred by day. The officer then proceeds at a slow pace along the line of the trench, the men following carefully in his footsteps. As soon as the last man reaches the starting point an officer or N.C.O. starts placing the men from the rear of the party, giving each man a task of two paces. Each time the officer halts the rear man unplaced falls in on the right of the officer and places his shovel in the ground beside the officers foot. The line of spades forms the trace of the trench and every man should at once spitlock his task making sure that the trace of the trench is preserved. A reliable N.C.O. should always follow the detailing officer and explain more fully to each man the nature of his task and check that the trace has been properly marked.

The best method of placing the men relatively to their task is shown in the diagram below

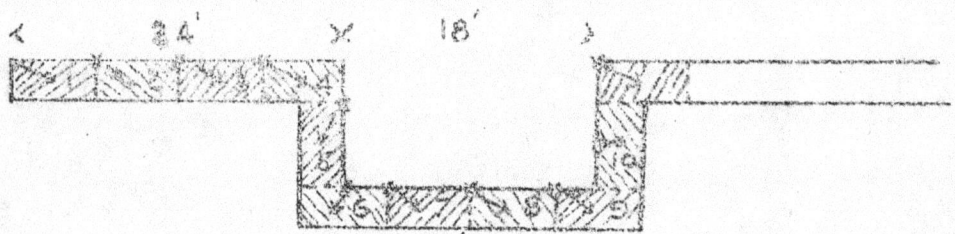

and everyone should keep this diagram in mind.

If the men are on the alert and jump to their places as soon as the officer halts the detailing can be done at the rate of one mile per hour; there is no congestion and the men themselves mark the general line for the detailing officer.

The one objection to this method of detailing is that the party is liable to get bunched up at the forward end and out of touch with the detailing officer. This can be got over by the leader going forward only the required distance - that is 14 paces for every 10 men of the working party and by the men being trained to keep a full arms length from the man in front.

C. CARRYING PARTIES. This training requires more attention than is generally given to it. All ranks must be trained to find their way in the dark - for which the North Star is of use. Men must be trained to keep touch and move quietly. A reliable N.C.O. should bring up the rear of the party to bring in stragglers and to act as guide should the party be cut in two. Men who show an aptitude for finding their way at night should be picked out. Leaders of parties must be careful to slow up after passing obstacle If the party is a big one a man with a pair of wire cutters and another with an axe are of great assistance.

D. WIRING will be carried out according to scheme taught at Third Army School. Material should as far as possible be made up in sets in one man loads. Particular stress should be laid on quietness or orderliness in working. As material will be scarce entanglements will have to be dismantled - still maintaining the drill and smartness.

The following system of wiring is suggested as an alternative to the 3rd Army School Instructions for use when men are scarce:-

The Unit working party is 7 men. These are divided into 2 groups - Picket Group and Wiring Group of 3 and 4 men respectively.

P.1 should be the N.C.O. or senior sapper in charge of the party - his duty is to lay out the pickets at the correct distance from the trench and at the proper intervals. The picket should always be placed flat on the ground with the point towards the enemy and over the exact spot where it is to be driven.

P.2 and 3 should be the tallest men of the party and practised in using a maul. P.2 holds the picket while P.3 strikes. As striking is tiring P.2 and 3 should be interchangeable. If screw pickets are used a tall man still has a distinct advantage.

W.3 and 4 carry the coil of barbed wire between them on a stick. They should have a pair of gloves between them to assist in loosening the wire should it become entangled on the coil. The duty of W.3 and 4 is to attach the end of their coil to a picket and run out the whole length of the coil on the ground at the foot of the pickets.

W.1 places the wire on the pickets with the assistance of W.2. W.2 will normally pick up the wire and place it against the picket whilst W.1 takes the turn and makes fast.

W.1 is head man of the wiring party and is responsible that the wiring is done as per instructions.

This system is applicable to all forms of wire entanglement including French wire.

3.

The first man to go out is P.1 carrying a few long pickets. He paces the required distance from the trench and places a picket. If the night is very dark he should arrange to have a luminous stick to assist him in keeping his direction.

P.2 and 3 follow after about 5 minutes and W.3,4, and 1,2, about 10 minutes later.

Each man should of course be told beforehand by the group commander in what order the pickets are to be placed and strands of wire put on. It will be found that the picket groups will finish about 20 min. to 15 min. before the wiring group. They can then employ themselves throwing loose wire into the entanglement.

A unit party will strongly wire 50 yards in two hours or can do 200 to 300 yards of S.A.Apron in a night.

It has been found the largest party which can work in the dark without falling over itself.

E. CONSOLIDATION will combine all the above. In digging trenches the following dimensions will be adhered to.

1) Fire bay - 24 feet, Traverse 18 feet wide.

2) The first relief of a fire trench will be 3'x3'x6' long. The second relief will widen to 5' at the top and deepen to 4'6" leaving a 1'6" fire step thus :-

[Diagram showing trench cross-section with "2nd RELIEF 51 c.ft." and "1st RELIEF 54 c.ft."]

During the first relief all excavated earth must be thrown forward and second relief back.

Communication trenches must always be started 5' wide at the top and kept 2'6" wide at the bottom.

Steps out every 50 yards will invariably be started with the third relief.

In digging men must be trained to work to a level bottom that is to never leave tell tales between tasks and never go deeper than the man on either side, as a trench which consists of a series of pits is instantly ruined by rain and is impossible to move along as it consists of 6' head cover in some places and 1' or 2' in other

Consolidation is usually carried out by means of a series of strong points for about one platoon each. It is quite impossible to lay down a design for a strong point as the trace depends so much on the contour of the ground, existing trenches, and dugouts, and the enemy. It must be left to the discretion of the officer in charge - but if he is in doubt the cross trench strong point shown in the sketch can always be used. It is easily dug in new ground or can be constructed from existing trenches or cross trenches with a little filling in and alterations. Frontal fire and flanking fire is obtained in all directions

There is a minimum amount of movement to man it against an attack in any direction and maximum concentration can be obtained in any one direction. Against an all round attack it is defendable with advantage to the defenders down to the last few men. It offers an indefinite target to artillery fire.

Firing grooves should be cut through each traverse to enable a man to fire down each bay should the enemy gain a footing in it. The design shown in the sketch gives a strong point for one platoon.

E. EXPLOSIVES. Opportunities should be taken to train certain men per section in explosives.

G. Officers will take every opportunity to give short lectures to their men on work carried out and future work.

H. The following are samples of orders given to the R.E. of the 17th Division, during recent operations on he SOMME. Each Brigade, in front line had O.C. and 1 section R.E. at Brigade H.Q., remaining 3 sections and Pioneers were in Divisional Reserve and practically under orders of C.R.E.

ORDERS - Extracts from

2/7/16   77th Fd. Co. R.E. will proceed tonight and make strong points at FRICOURT Farm, X.28.c.9.1.,X.28.d.7.3.,F.4.a.8.5. Arrangements will be made to reconnoitre before dark.
   2) One Coy Pioneers will be placed at disposal of O.C. 77th Fd. Co. R.E.
   3) 8 Wagons from 1st line transport will be allotted for stores.

3/7/16
   1) 77th Fd. Co. will make a strong point in CRUCIFIX trench about X.28.a.4.2.
   2) Clean and reverse CRUCIFIX Trench E. of X.28.a.4.2.in direction of Railway Copse turning back a flank towards X.28 Central.
   3) Carrying party of 200 strong from 6th Dorset Regt. will be provided.

5/7/16   Two sections of 93rd Fd. Co. R.E. will be placed at disposal of 52nd Brigade to form bombing steps in PEARL ALLEY etc.

8/7/16   77th Fd. Co. R.E. less 1 section and 1 Co. Pioneers will consolidate RAILWAY COPSE etc. etc., and repair 60 c.m. railway N. of Railway Copse.

The above give some idea of what were required of R.E.

Hdqrs,
  56th Divl. R.E.
    1/9/16.

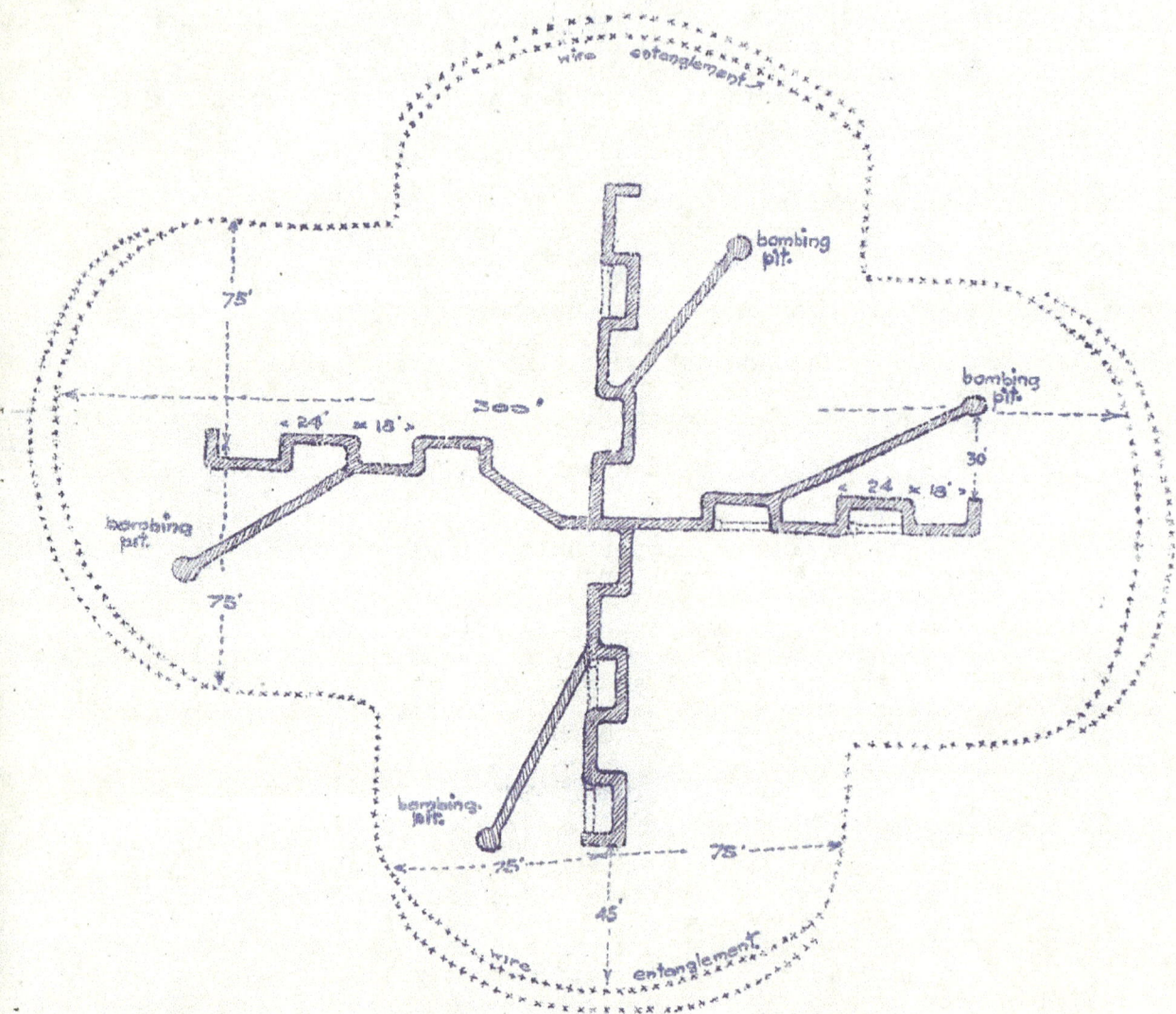

STRONGPOINT FOR A PLATOON
Approximate Scale. 50 Feet = 1 inch

OFFICE OF C.R.E.
56th DIVISIONAL ENGINEERS.

Appx B

REPORT on WORK of R.E. and PIONEERS of the

56th Division

- in -

SOMME Offensive

---

5 September 1916.   On this date the Division moved into the 14th Corps Reserve area with Headquarters at FORKED TREE. The 1/1st Edinburgh Field Co. R.E., the 2/1st London Field Co. R.E., and the 2/2nd London Field Co. R.E., with the 1/5th Cheshire Regiment (Pioneers) were bivouacked in HAPPY VALLEY, THE CITADEL and BOIS DE TAILLES.
Officers Commanding Field Companies were ordered to report to C.R.E., 5th Division to take over the work in progress, which they did at 9 p.m. on this day.

6th   "   "   On the 6th the 2/1st Field Co. started work on Advanced Brigade Headquarter Dugouts, working in section reliefs all round the clock.

7th   "   "   Divisional Headquarters moved to BILLON FARM, F.23.d.2.2.(62.D.N.E.) and the 3 Field Companies and the Pioneers moved into bivouacs about F.23.d.

The Edinburgh Field Co. started work on dugouts in German second line at about B.2.b.2.2. and the 2/2nd Field Co. on Brigade H.Q. dugouts at B.2.c.2.3.

2 Companies Pioneers started on digging C.T. from T.26.a.7.4. to a point S.E. of the W. corner of LEUZE WOOD.

8th   "   "   On this day a reconnaissance was made of forward tracks to ascertain work necessary to make them usable for horsed transport or cavalry in fair weather. Several tracks were sited using existing metalled cart tracks as far as possible.- Ground was found much cut up by shell holes.   On the same day the Pioneer Battalion started work on these in Company reliefs all round the clock.

9th   "   "   Work was started on 8 cut and cover dugouts for Divisional Battle H.Q. by the 2/1st Field Co.

On this date an attack was made by the 56th Division objectives being German positions from T.27.b.1.5½, to T.21.d.5½.2½. - T.21a.6.2½ - and T.31.a.8.2½ - T.15.c.1.4 - T.14.d.8½.4.   The 169th Infantry Brigade were ordered to establish S.P.s at T.27.b.1.5½., T.21.d.5½.2½., T.21.d.2.7 and T.21.d.1.9 and the 168th Brigade were to establish S.P.s at T.20.b.9.1., T.21.a.6.3., T.15.c.2.1., T.15.c.1.5 and T.14.d.9.4.   The objectives were not gained but considerable progress was made.

Night 9th/10th   Two sections of the 2/2nd Field Co. attached to 169 Brigade were employed in digging forward C.T. running N. of LEUZE WOOD (N.edge) and preparing trench running S.E. through that wood for defence.
The R.E. officer i/c these two sections was attached to 169 Brigade, and remained in close touch with Brigade H.Q. during the operations.

An officer of the 2/1st Co was similarly at disposal of 168th Brigade in case of necessity.

Fire trench was ordered to be dug from S. corner of

Night 9th/10th con:	LEUZE WOOD, T.27.a.2.4. to B.3.a.7.4. which was done by the Pioneers.
	Lieut. Beit (2/2nd Field Co) made a reconnaissance of the Northern end of BOULEAUX WOOD and found that enemy had made a block in the trench about 30 yards from the Eastern edge of the Wood and were still in the trench S.E. from the edge of the Wood and it was found essential to dig a C.T. to give connection with the captured line. This was done and by daybreak trench affording cover had been made.
10th Sep 1916.	The Pioneer Batt. of the 5th Division (Argyle & Sutherland Highlanders) came under my orders, and I gave directions for them to at at once get to work on the forward tracks. S.P.s were made during the day at T.21.d.1.9. and T.21.d.1.5.
11th " "	Work was continued by Pioneers on tracks and by the Field Companies on dugouts.
Night 11/12	Wiring was done by 2/1st Field Co. at T.15.c.0.5.
12th	Work continued on tracks and dugouts.
13th	Having received Div. Order 37 I called a conference of the O.s C. Companies and explained to them the work which would be required and what was expected in the forthcoming operations.
14th	I ordered the Field Companies to be in their battle areas by 5 a.m. on the 15th, to be located as follows: in Divisional Reserve:-

        2/1st London Field Co. ....A.12.a.
        2/2nd " " " .... A.11.a.
        1/1st Edinburgh " " ..... A.10.a.
        1/5th Cheshire Reg.(Pioneers) A.11.b.

and for the attack on the 15th they were attached as under:-
        Edinburgh Fd. Co. to   167th Inf. Brigade
        2/1st Fd. Co.   "   168th " "
        2/2nd Fd. Co   "   169th " "

and one Company Pioneers available every night for each Brigade in the line. The Field Co. of the Brigade in reserve and the Pioneers less 2 Companies were directly under the C.R.E. for work in rear.

15th	The offensive was resumed the Divisional objective being capture of MIDDLE COPSE and establishment of a strong protective flank E. and clear of BOULEAUX WOOD and to push forward to Railway N. thereof.
	I ordered the Field Co. and Pioneers to stand by for work on forward track from ANGLE WOOD to FALFEMONT FARM Spur through T.26.c.8.3., T.26.d.2.8., T.26.b.4.4., T.20.d.6.3., T.15.d.7.7., T.21.c.3.8., and T.21.a.7.5. thence along road to Railway Crossing, and later during the day I ordered this work to be proceeded with.
	Patrols were sent out frequently during the day to note condition of track, and its condition reported to Brigades.
Night 15/16.	As the Division had not gained all its objectives, an effort was made to consolidate positions held, but no great progres could be made as the points marked out for S.P.s were under shell fire by both sides, namely between MIDDLE COPSE and BOULEAUX WOOD.
	Work was however done on S.P. at T.27.b.1.4., which was wired on S. side. A new bombing block & entanglement in trench leading S. of S.P. was made - the bombing block

Night 15/16 con:	in LOOP Trench was improved and C.T. deepened and traverse commenced.
16/17 Sep.	Orders were received from Div. H.Q. that every effort must be made to consolidate. The 1/1st Edinburgh Fd. Co. (working under 169 Brigade) (a) Deepened trenches and improved S.P. at T.27.b.1.4. (b) Constructed wire entanglement 100 yards long on S. side of S.P. (c) Constructed new bombing block & entanglement in trench leading S. of S.P. to replace the one demolished. (d) Bombing block in LOOP TRENCH improved and C.T. deepened The Pioneers dug fore trench parallel to BOULEAUX WOOD from T.21.c.7.8. to T.21.c.9.8.
17/18 "	A preliminary reconnaissance was made at dusk of the position by Capt. Unwin R.E. and Lieut. Dain R.E.(2/2nd Fd. Co.) but owing to hostile activity it was not found possible to take sections out for work before 11 p.m. 2 Firebays were constructed across angle between LOOP TR. and C.T. dug by 1/5th Cheshires facing N.W. and 5 bays on an arc facing from N. to N.E. round the point of junction. 2 bays were also constructed across- in LOOP TRENCH to cover exposed flank of strong point bays. About 200 yards combined French and barbed wire entanglement was constructed Northwards from tank along front of LOOP TRENCH to W. face of S.P. Trenches 4'6" of cover 2 Companies of Pioneers attached to 167th Brigade constructed new C.T. at T.21a. - 125 yards long joining up partly dug C.T. with the old and new British lines The fire trench dug on previous night was deepened and completed. 1 Company Pioneers attached 169 Brigade dug trench from LOOP TRENCH at T.27.b.4.8. to T.21.c.9.3.
Day 18th & Night 18/19	Work was continued by day on tracks & by night on improvement of trenches.
Day 19th & Night 19/20	The Edinburgh Fd. Co. built 1st Aid Post at T.26.a.6.1. & completed Divisional Battle H.Q. dugouts whilst 1 section of that Company repaired bridges at CRUCIFIX. The 2/2nd Field Co. constructed (a) S.P. at T.27.b.4.8. consisting of 10 firebays on an arc from N.W. through N. to S. round junction of LOOP TRENCH & new trench parallel to sunken road. (b) S.P. consisting of 4 bays at T.27.c.7.8. across junction of assembly trench & FALFEMONT FARM Track. (c) 200 yards fire trench S.E. from T.27.c.7.8. to about T.27.d.1.6. All trenches were of an average depth of 4'6" to berm with firestep at intervals.
Day 20th	Pioneers cleared track 450 yards from WEDGE WOOD on GUILLEMONT ROAD.
Night 20/21	The 2/1st Fd. Co. completed 80 yards wiring E. of trench at MIDDLE COPSE (T.21.b.2.7.) The Pioneers dug 4 S.P.s in front of GROPI TRENCH.
Day 21	THE Pioneers continued work of clearing track from WEDGE WOOD to GUILLEMONT Cross Roads & completed a further 450 yds
Night 21/22	The Pioneers connected up the 4 S.P.s made the previous night by a traversed fire trench of a depth of 3'6" throughout with a depth of 4'6" in firebays. A C.T. was also dug connecting up 4 S.P.s to original front line.

4.

Day 22nd	Pioneers continued work of clearing track from WEDGE WOOD round North of cross roads E. of GUILLEMONT - road cleared and made good for a distance of 170 yards.

Night 22/23
Pioneers sapped from LOOP TRENCH forward to derelict tank, also improved S.P. at T.21.d. - firestep constructed where necessary & trench deepened. Work was also done on C.T. from LEUZEMAKE TRENCH to COMBLES TRENCH which was widened to 4'6" at top and 2'6" at bottom and deepened to 5' on a length of 129 yards.
One platoon Pioneers under 168th Brigade worked upon fire trench connecting S.P. at T.16.c.1.8. with S.P. South of it.

The 2/2nd Field Co. completed wiring S. of Sunken Road between S.P. at T.27.b.4.8. and LEUZE WOOD

The Edinburgh Field Co. put down 200 yards of H.W.E. in front of GROPI TRENCH & worked on C.T. from GROPI TRENCH to No. 1 Post.

Day 23rd & Night 23/24
Pioneers dug forward C.T. and connected up S.P.s
Track cleared from WEDGE WOOD to within 100 yards of GUILLEMONT Cross Roads & track marked out for tanks.

Edinburgh Field Co. erected H.W.E. covering No. 3 Post & wired 250 yards in BOULEAUX WOOD at T.21.c.8.7.

The 2/2nd Field Co. worked on 1st Cavalry Division Track.

Day 24th
Pioneers - Track from GUILLEMONT Cross Roads to LEUZE WOOD completed fit for guns & limbers & work commenced on new track

The 2/2nd Field Co. worked on making good 1st Cavalry Division Track.

Night 24/25
The pioneers dug out tank which was stuck in CHIMPANZEE ALLEY

The 2/2nd Field Co. constructed cut & cover splinter proof at T.27.c.1.5.

The Edinburgh Fd. Co. working under 168 Brigade
(A) Erected 80 yards H.W.E. to cover S.P. No. 3
(b) " 40 " entanglement in front of S.P. NO.2.
(c) Continued 2 dugouts at T.15.d.4.4. and with Advanced Brigade H.Q. at T.28.b.9.8.
(d) Wiring in BOULEAUX WOOD at T.21.c.8.7. on a front of 250 yards.

25th
The attack was resumed on enemy position, the Divisional objectives being (a) to secure fire position N. corner of BOULEAUX WOOD and obtain touch with 5th Division about T.16.c. 4½.7. Two Sections 2/1st London Field Co. and 1 Co. Pioneers were placed at disposal of 168th Brigade for consolidation.

Night 25/26
The 2/1st Field Co. made S.P.s as follows:-
(a) T.16.c.5.6.) 210 yards wired in a semicircle facing S.
(b) T.16.c.4.7.)
(c) T.16.c.0.2.) 120 yards one bay deep facing S.W.,
) partly in wood.
(d) T.16.c.3.1. 65 yards one bay deep facing S.E.

Whilst the Pioneers made SP.s. each to contain 50 men as follows:-

Night 25/26 T.15.d.9.0.
con; T.16.c.3½.0.
  T.16.c.4.4.
  T.16.c.3.7.

26th   The 2/2nd Field Co. continued work on 1st Cavalry Track
        and dug-outs.

        The Pioneers worked in continuous relief's on road ANGLE WOOD
        to COMBLES - the whole length being made good.

        The 2/2nd Field Co. made track from ANGLE WOOD to FALFEMONT
        FARM for water carts, a graded track being cut in hillside
        at B.2.c.4.2. joining FALFEMONT FARM Road about B.2.c.5.5.
        The track was completed by 11 p.m.

Army Form C.

Vol 9
H.Q. 56 J Div R E

WAR DIARY
or
INTELLIGENCE SUMMARY
(Erase heading not required.)

Instructions regarding War Diaries and Intelligence Summaries are contained in F.S. Regs., Part II. and the Staff Manual respectively. Title Pages will be prepared in manuscript.

Place	Date	Hour	Summary of Events and Information	Remarks and references to Appendices
Battle HQ	1/10/16		Received 56th Div. S.G. 1387/5 – giving alterations in Divisional boundaries. Visited Field Companies + discussed work being done	
"	2/10/16		Received Operation Order No 51 – Issued Order for relief of 2/2 Field Co by 2/1st Field Co	
"	3/10/16		Received D.S.O. 53 ordering reorganisation of offensive on 3rd inst – interviewed O's C. Companies in connection therewith	
"	4/10/16		Received O.C. 1st tel. giving detail of Dugouts required by 4th Division	
"	5/10/16		C.R.E. visited Dressing Station + dug outs being worked on by Companies	
"	6/10/16		Received Div. Order 53 reinforcing operation ordered by No 52 – The 2/1 London F.C. being allotted with 1/1 L.G. Pioneers to 168 Infantry Brigade + the Edinburgh F.C. + 1 company Pioneers being allotted to 167 Infantry Brigade	
"	7/10/16		Received Div Order 54 ordering attack to be renewed tomorrow –	

WAR DIARY or INTELLIGENCE SUMMARY

Army Form C. 2118

HQ 51st Divn R.E.

Place	Date	Hour	Summary of Events and Information	Remarks and references to Appendices
Battle HQ.	8/10/16		Recd D.O. 55. That Division would be relieved on night 9/10 by 4th Divn. Bygrove handing over Subsequent. Conference with C.R.E. 4th Divn. & Adjutant explaining works in progress. Issued Orders to Field Companies regarding relief.	
"	9/10/16		Received D.O. 56. Handed over to C.R.E. 4th Division. Moved from Battle HQ. to Citadel. Issued Warning Order to Field Companies in regard to probable further moves.	
CITADEL	10/10/16		Received Order in regard to date for movement of personnel by bus. Orders issued to Field Companies in accordance therewith.	
YZEUX	11/10/16		HQ. moved to YZEUX by motorbus.	
"	12/10/		Transport arrived. Consultation with O.s. C. Companies, drawing up programme for steady training for every morning of next period. Laon Shooting orders issued.	
"	13/10			

Army Form C. 2.

WAR DIARY
or
INTELLIGENCE SUMMARY

(Erase heading not required.)

Instructions regarding War Diaries and Intelligence Summaries are contained in F. S. Regs, Part II. and the Staff Manual respectively. Title Pages will be prepared in manuscript.

Place	Date	Hour	Summary of Events and Information	Remarks and references to Appendices
YZEUX	14/10		Weeks Programme drawn up	
"	15/10		C.R.E. went on leave – Training continued	
"	16/10		Training continued	
"	17/10		Do. Warning Order received that Division would move	
"	18/10		to HALLENCOURT AREA.	
"			Received D.O. No 57 ordering move.	
"	19/10		Preparing for move.	
"	20/10		Left for HALLENCOURT – Arrived 11-30 a.m. – Received billeting instructions in regard to new area	
HALLENCOURT	21/10		Received Preliminary Notes on our move to the Sector about to be taken over	
			Received Divisional Order No 58 –	
	22/10		Adjutant left for LES TRETS & visited C.R.E., 6th Division & received with their outstanding works, method of drawing stores & the purpose along to taking over.	

1875 Wt. W593/826 1,000,000 4/15 J.B.C. & A. A.D.S.S./Forms/C. 2118.

WAR DIARY
or
INTELLIGENCE SUMMARY
(Erase heading not required.)

Army Form C. 2118.

Instructions regarding War Diaries and Intelligence Summaries are contained in F. S. Regs., Part II. and the Staff Manual respectively. Title Pages will be prepared in manuscript.

Place	Date	Hour	Summary of Events and Information	Remarks and references to Appendices
HALLENCOURT	23/10		Adjutant worked Left Sector of Line & Divisional dumps in new area —	
	24/10		H.Q. left 12 night to entrain at LONGPRÉ — Received D.O. No 69 —	
LONG-PRÉ MANVILLE LESTREM	25/10		Entraining at LONGPRÉ 5 hours late — arrangements there most trying — up to date — only 1 ramp for entraining all Hy. horses — arrived Merville 4pm — arrived LESTREM — 6pm	
"	26/10		2 O.R's returned from leave	
"	"		Issued R.E Grignon Order (Appendix +) Adjutant visited centre sector of new line	+
"	27/10		Day spent in going through placements maps & records with Adjutant 61st Division preparatory to taking over	
LA GORGUE	28/10		Companies moved — Took over from C.R.E. 61st Div'n	
	29/10/		C.R.E. visited front line — engaged all day — Adjutant ill — No signature received that Engineer Stores had been evacuated for a commence'm to was to proceed to England —	

WAR DIARY or INTELLIGENCE SUMMARY

Army Form C.2118

F.Q. 56th Div't R.E

Place	Date	Hour	Summary of Events and Information	Remarks and references to Appendices
LA GORGUE	31/10		C.R.E visited right sector of line - met O/c 2/2nd Lond. O - discussed works in progress.	
	31/10		Capt & Adj't. J.H. Green R.E sent to Hospital. Intelligent measures that draughtsman appointed to Commission in 5th Lt Surrey C - Serj't Matthews 2/1 London Lond. O reported to take up duties of Engineer Clerk Sergeant.	
			Generally With regard to the short rest period spent at YZEUX I consider that we all rest periods Divisional Engineers should if possible be billeted together - A Junior N.C.O's class was formed out of the 3 Companies. Each morning was instructed by the R.S.M in discipline & military matters - by this means a marked improvement was noticed in these N.C.O.s	

2/11/16

Jas Tuder
Lt Col RE
C.R.E 56 Div.

SECRET.   Copy No. 2...

R.E. OPERATION ORDER No. 1.

1. The 56th. Division less Divnl. Artillery are relieving the 61st. Divn. on 27th and 28th October in the left sector XIth Corps as follows:-
   169th Inf. Bde. relieve 183rd Inf. Bde. in NEUVE CHAPELLE Sect.
   167th. "   "   "   184th "   "   in MOATED GRANGE Sect.
   168th. "   "   "   182nd "   "   in FAUQUISSART Sect.
2. The disposition of Bde. H.Q. and Battalions on nights of 26/27th to 29/30th Octr. are shown on attached Table "A".
3. R.E. and Pioneers will carry out reliefs on the 28th inst. as shown on attached Table "B". Headquarters to be established as shown on column "3" of that table.
   Reliefs to be commenced at 7am. on 28th. inst. and to be completed by 5-30pm. Completion of relief to be reported by wire.
4. R.E. Headquarters will move to LA GORGUE on the 28th inst., and will be established there at 3-30pm. on that day.
5. Relieving Units will submit to this office by 12noon on the 29th. inst. lists of all dump and trench stores taken over by them, and schedule of maps, defence schemes etc handed over to them, and furnish location of any workshops taken over.
6. The 3 Field Coys. and the Pioneers will arrange for cyclist orderlies to attend daily at R.E. Headquarters at 10am and 4pm. commencing on the afternoon of the 28th inst.
7. Ingoing Units will on relief satisfy themselves that no claims for damage or rent are outstanding in respect of the premises taken over.
8. Acknowledge.

                                        (Sd) H.W.Gordon, Lt. Col.R.E
                                             C. R. E., 56th. Division.

Headquarters, 56th. Divnl. R.E.,
25th. October, 1916.

Distribution.

Copy No. 1 to 2/1st. London Fd. Co., R.E.
  "   " 2 to 2/2nd.   "   "   "   "
  "   " 3 to 1/1st. City of Edinr. Fd. Co.
  "   " 4 to 1/5th. Cheshire Regt.
  "   " 5 to 56th. Divn. (G)
  "   " 6 to   "   "   (Q)
  "   " 7 to C.R.E., 61st Divn.
  "   " 8 to War Diary.
  "   " 9 to File.

Table "A"

DISPOSITIONS OF BRIGADE H.Q. and BATTALIONS on NIGHTS 26/27th to 29/30th October issued with 56th Divisional Order No. 59.

Brigade.	Night 26/27th.	Night 27/28th.	Night 28/29th.	Night 29/30th.
169th.	Bde. H.Q. CALONNE.	Bde. H.Q. CALONNE.	Bde.H.Q. LES HUIT MAISONS. (R.30.c.5.9.)	Bde. H.Q. LES HUIT MAISONS. 2 Bns. line NEUVE CHAPELLE Section.
	1 Bn. FOSSE.	1 Bn. FOSSE.	1 Bn. FOSSE.	
	1 Bn. LESTREM. 1 Bn. L'EPINETTE PARADIS.	1 Bn. LESTREM. 1 Bn. CROIX BARBEE.	1 Bn. LESTREM. 1 Bn. CROIX BARBEE.	1 Bn. CROIX BARBEE. 1 Bn. BOUT DELVILLE.
	1 Bn. CALONNE.	1 Bn. BOUT DELVILLE.	2 Bns. line NEUVE CHAPELLE Sect.	
167th.	Bde. H.Q. LA GORGUE.	Bde. H.Q. LA GORGUE.	Bde. H.Q. COCKSHY HOUSE. (M.9.b.8.9.)	Bde. H.Q. COCKSHY HOUSE.
	2 Bns. LA GORGUE.	2 Bns. LA GORGUE.	2 Bn. LA GORGUE.	2 Bns. line MOATED GRANGE Section.
	1 Bn. ROBERMETZ.	2 Bns. RIEZ BAILLEUL.	2 Bns. line MOATED GRANGE Sect.	2 Bns. RIEZ BAILLEUL.
	1 Bn. to Gd. PACAUT.			
168th.	Bde. H.Q. ESTAIRES.	Bde. H.Q. ESTAIRES.	Bde. H.Q. LAVENTIE. N.4.b.2.6.	Bde. H.Q. LAVENTIE.
	4 Bns. ESTAIRES.	2 Bns. ESTAIRES. 2 Bns. LAVENTIE.	2 Bns. ESTAIRES. 2 Bns. line FAUQUISSART Section.	2 Bns. line FAUQUISSART Sect. 2 Bns. LAVENTIE.

Head Qrs., 56th Divn.
24th. October, 1916.

(sd) J. Brind, Lieut. Col.,
General Staff.

TABLE "B".

1. UNIT.	2. Relieves	3. H.Q. at	REMARKS.
2/1st. London Field Co. R.E.	1/3rd. South Midland Field Co.	M.4.c.9.6. LAVENTIE.	
2/2nd. London Field Co. R.E.	2/2nd. do.	R.29.b.3.7. HUIT MAISONS.	
1/1st. City of Edinr. Fd. Co.	3/1st. do.	M.9.b.6.9. LAVENTIE.	
1/5th. Cheshire Regt. (Pioneers)	1/5th. D.C.L.I.	M.4.d.4.6. LAVENTIE.	"

Head Qrs., 56th Divisional R.E.   (Sd) H.W.Gordon, Lieut. Col., R.E.,
25th. October, 1916.   C.R.E., 56th. Division.

Army Form C. 21

WAR DIARY
INTELLIGENCE SUMMARY.
Hdqrs. 56th Divl. R.E.

(Erase heading not required.)

Instructions regarding War Diaries and Intelligence Summaries are contained in F. S. Regs., Part II. and the Staff Manual respectively. Title pages will be prepared in manuscript.

Vol 10

Place	Date	Hour	Summary of Events and Information	Remarks and references to Appendices
	1916			
LA GORGUE	1/11		Staff Captain of C.E. XI Corps called to discuss the works in hand. Visited right sector of line.	
"	2/11		O/c 2/1st London Field C.R.E. called to receive instructions. O/c 1/5th Cheshire Regt called & discussed arrangements made for disposition of R.Es. and Powers and allocation of work.	
"	3/11		Visited left sector with O/c 2/1st London Field C.R.E. C.E. XI Corps saw me with reference to the general work of the Division. Attended Divisional Conference at 168th Brigade Hdqrs.	
"	4/11		O/c C.E. XI Corps in the afternoon.	
"	6/11		Went round front line with 1st Army Commander.	
"	7/11		R/c Seq's left for England	
"	8/11		Visited positions with "Camel Officer". Visited front line, centre sector.	
"	9/11		Visited front line, left sector.	
"	11/11		Had the O.C. Field Coys in to discuss the work in hand.	
"	15/11		Visited right sector of front line.	

Army Form C. 2118.

WAR DIARY
INTELLIGENCE SUMMARY.
Hdq/rs, 56th Divn R.E.

(Erase heading not required.)

Place	Date	Hour	Summary of Events and Information	Remarks and references to Appendices
LA GORGUE	17/11		Visited Centre sector of front line.	
"	18/11		Visited left sector of front line.	
"	20/11		Went round front line with G.O.C. of the Division.	
"	23/11		Visited Centre sector of front line.	
"	24/11		Went round the front with C.R.E. 5th Division.	
"	25/11		Received Std Order No 60 & Issued Order No CR/S.344, copy attached.	A
"			Visited right sector of line.	
"	26/11		The O.C. Field Coys attended to discuss the redistribution of the Corps line.	
"			Received SG.351 (Addition to Std Order 60) & AQS/160 (Administrative Instructions 6 Divn)	
"	27/11		Visited right sector of line.	
"	28/11		Visited NEUVE CHAPELLE.	
"	29/11		Issued continuation to CR/S.344, also a revised table of reliefs.	B & C
"	30/11		Visited left sector of line.	

2/12/16.

Jas Brown
Lt Col R.E.
C.R.E. 56th Divn

Appendix A *Copy No 9*

56th DIVISIONAL ENGINEERS ORDER No. CR/S 374.

1. There will be a redistribution of the XIth Corps line.

2. The 56th Division will hand over to the 5th Division the portion of the line between BOND STREET (S.10.c.28.05.) and CHURCH ROAD (S.5.a.-92.22.)

3. The Southern Boundary of 56th Division will be point S.5.a.92.22. thence along CHURCH ROAD (inclusive to 56th Division) to S.5.a.41.65. - M.34.c.8.7. thence to CROIX BARBEE (exclusive to 56th Division) - HUITMAISON (inclusive to 56th Division, but present Headquarters of 169th Infantry Brigade will be at disposal of 5th Division.) - thence to FOSSE (exclusive to 56th Division) and across to old boundary at R.13.d.4.1. CHURCH ROAD Communication Trench will be used by both 56th and 5th Divisions.

4. The Division will hold the new front with two Brigades in the line and one in reserve. The boundary line between Brigades will be a line through points M.24.c.8.2. - M.24.c.35.75. to a point M.23.b.8.5., where it joins and follows the existing inter-Brigade boundary.

5. The Divisional R.E., will have three companies in the line. The distribution of R.E.Pioneers permanent working parties will continue to be as at present.

6. The Field Companies will work on fronts as follows :-

    2/1st London Fd.Co. R.E., BOND STREET to DRURY LANE (both inclusive.)
    1/1st Edinburgh Fd.Co.R.E., DRURY LANE (exclusive) to TILLELOY SOUTH (exclusive.)
    2/2nd London Fd.Co.R.E., TILLELOY SOUTH to CHURCH ROAD (both inclusive)

The exact boundary between Field Company Sectors will depend on Battalion boundaries and will be notified later.

7. Field Companies and Pioneers will remain in billets as at present.

8. Field Companies will re-arrange Advanced Dumps according to requirements.

9. Field Companies will take over their new Sectors by midnight 27/28th November.

10. Completion of relief to be notified to this Office.

Issued at 7-20p.m.
24/11/16.

                                          Lieut.Col.R.E.,
                                          C.R.E.56th Division.

Copy Nos.
1. 2/1st London Fd.Co.   6. 168th Brigade.
2. 1/1st Edinburgh Fd.Co.   7. 169th Brigade.
3. 2/2nd London Fd.Co.   8. "G"
4. 1/5th Cheshire Regt.   9. War Diary.
5. 167th Brigade.   10. C.R.E., 5th Division.

Appendix C

Revised Table of Reliefs.

The two R.E., sections in the line in each Field Coy. sector will be relieved by the two sections R.E. in reserve every 12 days, corresponding with Battalion and Brigade reliefs.

The day of the relief ie:- from 6-0am. of the day of relief to 6-0am. following day will be observed by each Company as a rest day for Company Parades and Recreation. Only very urgent work will be carried out on this day, and any men then working should be given a day's rest at the earliest opportunity.

Each man may at the discretion of the O.C. Company be given one half day off duty between each relief.

From their sections in reserve each Company will provide one section for Tramways, Nouveau Monde or Divisional School, Merville according to the following programme:-

12 day relief commencing.	Nouveau Monde.	Tramways.	Merville.
Novr. 28th.	2/2.	2/1.	E.
Decr. 10th.	2/1.	E.	2/2.
" 22nd.	E.	2/2.	2/1.
Jan. 3rd.	2/2.	2/1.	E.
" 15th.	2/1.	E.	2/2.
" 27th.	E.	2/2.	2/1.

The dates given above may vary slightly according to Infantry reliefs.

The section on detachment will rejoin it's Company after work, on the day before the relief and the section taking over will arrive in time for the day's work on the day after the relief.

This arrangement is made for the convenience of Companies so that the whole Company can be together on Rest day, but O.C's must see to it that the work in the back area does not suffer ie:- sections must arrive in good time for work, and the Section Officers must carefully take over all work from the outgoing section.

One man from both the outgoing and incoming sections will remain over the relief day in the section billets as Guard, to prevent the billets being taken by any other Unit.

Capt.R.E., & Adjt.,
for C.R.E. 56th Division.

29/11/16.

Copy Nos. 1. 2/1st London Fd.Co.R.E.   5. War Diary.
          2. 2/2nd London Fd.Co.R.E.   6. 167 Brigade.
          3. 1/1st Edinburgh Fd.Co.R.E. 7. 168 Brigade.
          4. C.R.E.   8. 169 Brigade.
                9. 1/5th Cheshire Regiment.

Appendix B

Continuation of

56th DIVISIONAL ENGINEERS ORDER No. CR/S 374.

The boundaries between Field Company sectors for the front line system will be as follows:-

DRURY LANE and STRAND (inclusive to 2/1st London Fd.Co.) back to RUE BACQUERET.
TILLELOY S. (inclusive to 2/2nd London Fd.Co.) " " " "

All work in these areas will be undertaken by the respective Field Companies under arrangements with the Brigades.

Headquarter units of the two Brigades in the line will obtain their R.E., stores and technical assistance as follows:-

RIGHT SECTOR.
Right Infantry Brigade Headquarters.	- 1/1st Edinburgh Fd.Co.R.E.
Right Battalion Headquarters.	- 2/2nd London Fd.Co.R.E.
Left Battalion Headquarters.	- 1/1st Edinburgh Fd.Co.R.E.
Support Battalion Headquarters.	- 2/2nd London Fd.Co.R.E.
Reserve Battalion.	- 2/2nd London Fd.Co.R.E.
M.G.Company.	- 1/1st Edinburgh Fd.Co.R.E.
T.M.Battery.	- 1/1st Edinburgh Fd.Co.R.E.

LEFT SECTOR.
Left Infantry Brigade Headquarters.	- 2/1st London Fd.Co.R.E.
Right Battalion Headquarters.	- 1/1st Edinburgh Fd.Co.R.E.
Left Battalion Headquarters.	- 2/1st London Fd.Co.R.E.
Support Battalion Headquarters.	- 2/1st London Fd.Co.R.E.
Reserve Battalion.	- 2/1st London Fd.Co.R.E.
M.G.Company.	- 2/1st London Fd.Co.R.E.
T.M.Battery.	- 2/1st London Fd.Co.R.E.

RESERVE BRIGADE. (all units.) — C.R.E.

TRANSPORT LINES. (all units.) — O.i/c Horse Stdgs. c/o C.R.E.

DIVISIONAL ARTILLERY.
Right Group.	- 2/2nd London Fd.Co.R.E.
Centre Group.	- 1/1st Edinburgh Fd.Co.R.E.
Left Group.	- 2/2nd London Fd.Co.R.E.
D.A.C.	- C.R.E.

DIVISIONAL TRAIN. — C.R.E.

A.D.M.S. — C.R.E.

Advanced Dressing Station,	Laventie.	- 2/1st London Fd.Co.R.E.
do do do	La Flinque.	- 1/1st Edinburgh Fd.Co.R.E.
do do do	Green Barn.	- 2/2nd London Fd.Co.R.E.

MISCELLANEOUS. (as per location table AQS/5.) — C.R.E.

All applications for stores must state against each item the purpose for which it is required.

In the case of new work, a short scheme with sketches of what is required should be submitted.

The scheme should be accompanied by a short reason as to why the new work has become necessary.

Lieut.Col.R.E.,
C.R.E. 56th Division.

Issued 4-30pm.
29/11/16.

Copy Nos.
1. 2/1st London Fd.Co.
2. 2/2nd London Fd.Co.
3. 1/1st Edinburgh Fd.Co.
4. 1/5th Cheshire Regiment.
5. 167 Brigade.
6. 168 Brigade.
7. 169 Brigade.
8. "G"
9. A.D.M.S.
10. Divnl. Artillery.
11. " Train.
12. War Diary.

Army Form C. 2118.

WAR DIARY
INTELLIGENCE SUMMARY.
(Erase heading not required.)

Hdqrs. 56th Div R.E.

Vol XI

Place	Date	Hour	Summary of Events and Information	Remarks and references to Appendices
	1916			
LA GORGUE	2/12		Visited left sector of line	
"	4/12		Visited right sector of line	
"	5/12		Attended conference at XI Corps Hdqtrs. Received 56th Div Order No. 61.	
"	6/12		Visited left sector of line	
"	9/12		Visited right sector of line	
"	11/12		Visited left sector of line	
"	12/12		Visited right sector of line	
"	14/12		C.R.E. left for England on 5 days special leave. Major GT KINGSFORD arrived as acting CRE	
"	15/12		The Adjutant attended conference at Div Hdqtrs. Received 56th Div Order No. 62	
"	17/12		Issued Order No. 75 Copy attached	A
"	18/12		Received continuation of 56th Div Order No. 62	
"	19/12		C.R.E. 37 Divis. called to discuss the taking over of the sector between CHURCH RD (exclusive) and SIGN POST LANE (exclusive) by that Divis.	
"	20/12		C.R.E. returned from leave	

WAR DIARY
INTELLIGENCE SUMMARY.

Hdqtrs 56th Div R.E.

(Erase heading not required.)

Place	Date	Hour	Summary of Events and Information	Remarks and references to Appendices
	1916			
LA GORGUE	21/12		Visited front line	
"	22/12		Issued Contination to Order No 75. Copy attd.	B
"	23/12		Visited C.E. XI Corps.	
"	24/12		Visited front line with C.R.E. 39th Divn	
"	26/12		Visited front line	
"	27/12		Visited front line	
"	28/12		Visited front line	
"	29/12		Visited front line	
"	30/12		Received 56th Divn Order No 63. Issued Order No 76. Copy attd.	C
"			Visited front line	

2/1/17

J.S. Foreman
Lieut Col R.E.
C.R.E. 56th Divn

56th. DIVISIONAL ENGINEERS ORDER No. 75.

1. The following reliefs will take place on the 21st December.

   (a) Portion of 169th Infantry Brigade in NEUVE CHAPELLE Section between CHURCH ROAD (exclusive) and SIGN POST LANE (exclusive) by "A" Brigade 37th Division.

   (b) Portion of 168th Infantry Brigade in FAUQUISSART Section between present brigade boundary and BRITE STREET (inclusive) by 169th Infantry Brigade.

   (c) Portion of 168th Infantry Brigade in FAUQUISSART Section between BRITE STREET (exclusive) and BOND STREET (inclusive) by 167th Infantry Brigade.

   (d) The 2/2nd London Fd.Co. will hand over to a Field Company of the 37th Division all works in hand and stores between the present Divisional boundary at CHURCH ROAD and a line from junction of SIGN POST LANE with FRONT LINE - SIGN POST LANE (exclusive to 37th Division) - N.27.b.25.65. - N.20.c.5.7. as well as SUSSEX DEEP and billets and workshops at ROUF MAISONS.

2. On relief, the 2/2nd London Fd.Co. will move into billets at the Racing Stables LAVENTIE. O.C. 1/1st Edinburgh Fd.Co. will arrange to hand over half the accommodation of those billets.

12/12/16.

Capt. .., & Adjt.,
for C.R.E., 56th Division.

1. 2/1st London Fd.Co.R.E.
2. 2/2nd London Fd.Co.R.E.
3. 1/1st Edinburgh Fd.Co.R.E.
4. "A"
5. War Diary.

56th Divisional Engineers Order No. 76.

1. The 168th Infantry Brigade will relieve the 169th Infantry Brigade in the MOATED GRANGE Section on the 2nd and 3rd January 1917, the relief to be completed by 6-0 am on 3rd January.

2. The relief of the Section at MERVILLE and NOUVEAU MONDE will take place on 2nd January, to be completed by 9-30 am on 3rd January.

3. More attention must be paid this time to the handing over of Sections at MERVILLE and NOUVEAU MONDE.

29/12/16.

Capt. R.E. & Adjt.
for C.R.E., 56th Division.

Copy No. 1   2/1st London Field Coy R.E.
        2   2/2nd London Field Coy R.E.
        3   1/1st Edinburgh Field Coy R.E.
        4   "G"
        5   War Diary.

In continuation of

56th DIVISIONAL ENGINEERS ORDER No.75.

1. In continuation of Divisional R.E. Order No.75.

   The boundaries between Field Company Sections will be as follows:-

   (a) Between 2/1st London Fd.Co. and 1/1st Edinburgh Fd.Co.
       Drury Lane and Strand inclusive to 1/1st Edinburgh Fd.Co.
   (b) Between 1/1st Edinburgh Fd.Co. and 2/2nd London Fd.Co.
       Winchester Avenue inclusive to 2/2nd London Fd.Co.

2. As regards the issuing of stores and the supervision of work for the garrison of the trenches, these boundaries may be varied to correspond to the nearest Infantry Company boundaries.

3. The Midland Railway will be used by both 1/1st Edinburgh Fd.Co. and 2/2nd London Fd.Co.

4. The responsibility for Artillery work will remain as at present is:-

222nd. Bde. R.F.A.	-	2/2nd London Fd.Co.
280th. " "	-	1/1st Edinburgh Fd.Co.
281st. " "	-	2/1st London Fd.Co.

22/12/15.

Capt.R.E., & Adjt., for
C.R.E., 56th Division.

1. 2/1st London Fd.Co.R.E.
2. 2/2nd London Fd.Co.R.E.
3. 1/1st Edinburgh Fd.Co.R.E.
4. "G".
5. War Diary.

Army Form C. 2118.

Hdqrs, 56th Divn F.C.

Vol 12

WAR DIARY
INTELLIGENCE SUMMARY.
(Erase heading not required.)

Instructions regarding War Diaries and Intelligence Summaries are contained in F.S. Regs., Part II. and the Staff Manual respectively. Title pages will be prepared in manuscript.

Place	Date	Hour	Summary of Events and Information	Remarks and references to Appendices
	1917			
LA GORGUE	1/1		Visited front line	
"	2/1		Visited front line	
"	3/1		Visited front line	
"	4/1		Visited front line	
"	5/1		Visited Special Works Park, WIMEREAUX	
"	6/1		Visited front line	
"	8/1		Visited 168th Brigade & on to front line	
"	10/1		Visited front line. Had O.C. Coys in to look over work in hand	
"	11/1		Visited LAVENTIE & on to front line	
"	12/1		Attended Conference at C.E's Office XI Corps	
"	13/1		Received 56th Divn Order No 64 & issued Order No 79 Copy attd."	A
"	13/1		Visited front line	
"	14/1		Attended Conference at C.E's Office XI Corps	
"	15/1		Visited front line	
"	16/1		Visited front line; also R.E. Workshops.	
"	18/1		Visited front line	

Army Form C. 2118.

WAR DIARY

INTELLIGENCE SUMMARY.
(Erase heading not required.)

Instructions regarding War Diaries and Intelligence
Summaries are contained in F.S. Regs., Part II.
and the Staff Manual respectively. Title pages
will be prepared in manuscript.

Place	Date	Hour	Summary of Events and Information	Remarks and references to Appendices
	1917			
LA GORGUE	18/1		Visited front line	
"	19/1		Visited front line	
"	23/1		Received 56 Field Order No. 65 & issued order No. 78 copy attached	B
"	24/1		Capt. D.H. GREEN M.C.R.E. left to take over command of 59th Field Co.R.E. Lieut. J.T.F. HENDERSON, 2/1st London Field Co.R.E. appointed Adjutant.	
"	25/1		Visited front line. The Acting Visited the Barrows Workshop.	
"	28/1		Conference with the O.C. Field Coys at 2/1st London Field Co. Hqrs. as to the rearranging of front line on 39th Divn leaving the Corps.	
"	30/1		Visited front line	

4/2/17

F. Myays
Lt Col
a/C.R.E. 56 Divsion

Major R.E.
56 Divsion

Secret

56th Divisional Engineers Order No.77.

1. The 169th Infantry Brigade will relieve the 167th Infantry Brigade in the FAUQUISSART Section on the 14th January, 1917, the relief to be completed by midnight 14th.

2. The relief of the Sections at MERVILLE and NOUVEAU MONDE will take place on 14th January, to be completed by 8-30am on 15th January.

11/1/17.

Capt.R.E., & Adjt.,for
C.R.E., 56th.Division.

Copies Nos. 1. 2/1st London Field Co.R.E.
             2. 2/2nd London Field Co.R.E.
             3. 1/1st Edinburgh Field Co.R.E.
             4. War Diary.

SECRET.

56th DIVISIONAL ENGINEERS Order No.78.

1. The 167th Infantry Brigade will relieve the 168th Infantry Brigade in the MOATED GRANGE Section on the 26th January, the relief to be complete by midnight 26/27th.

2. The relief of the Sections at MERVILLE and NOUVEAU MONDE will take place on 26th January, to be completed by 8-30am. on 27th January.

23/1/17.

Capt.R.E., & Adjt.,
for C.R.E., 56th.Division

Copies Nos. 1. 2/1st London Fd.Co.R.E.
             2. 2/2nd London Fd.Co.R.E.
             3. 1/1st Edinburgh Fd.Co.R.E.
             4. War Diary.

SECRET.

SECRET.   Copy No. 8

R.E. Operation Order No.79.

1. The 56th Division extend their front and relieve the 37th
   Division in the Neuve Chapelle section from Sign Post Lane
   to Bond St on the 1st. and 2nd. February.

2. The 513 (London) Field Company R.E. will relieve the 152
   Field Company and take over billets at 8 Maisons under arrangements to be made direct between Officers Commanding. Relief to
   be completed by daylight 3rd February.
   All work, dumps, stores etc, will be taken over by evening of
   2nd February.

3. The two platoons 1/5th Cheshire Regiment working in the right
   section will take over billets from O.C. "C" Company N.Stafford
   Regiment at CROIX BARBEE M.26.d.5.5. Relief to be completed
   by daylight 3rd February.

4. The Southern Boundary of the 56th Division will be Bond St. S.
   - S.9.a.9.6. - S.9.d.4.4. M.32.d.6.3. M.31.a.0.0. all
   inclusive to 56th Division.

5. Completion of relief to be reported to this office.

6. ACKNOWLEDGE.

                                                    [signature]
                                                    Lieut.Col.R.E.
31/1/17.   C.R.E., 56th. Division.

Distribution.

    Copy Nos. 1.   2/1st London Fd.Co.   512 F² Coy
              2.   2/2nd London Fd.Co.   513   "   "
              3.   1/1st Edinburgh Fd.Co. 416 "   "
              4.   1/5th Cheshire Regiment.
              5.   Headquarters, "G"
              6.   "   "Q"
              7.   C.R.E., 37th Division.
              8.   War Diary.
              9.   File.

WAR DIARY
INTELLIGENCE SUMMARY

(Erase heading not required.)

Army Form C. 2118

AQ RE 5-6 D

Vol 13

Place	Date	Hour	Summary of Events and Information	Remarks and references to Appendices
LA GORGUE	1917 23/2		Major F.G.P. GEDGE returned to unit. Issued Order No 80. Copy attached. Reccyed SK WO Order 68. Boundaries of the Divisions consequent to taking over part of the 51st Div front. The rearrangement will take place from 26 to 29 Feb: and Orders No 81 has been issued. Copy attd.	A
	24/2		Visited front line	B
	27/2		Received 56" Order No 69. Visited front line. Issued Order No 82. Copy attached. C.R.E. 49th Div arrived. Advanced HQ work in progress	C
	28/2		Visited front line with the C.R.E. 49th Div.	

4/3/17

Jas Jordan
Lieut Col RE
C.R.E. 56 Div

WAR DIARY or INTELLIGENCE SUMMARY

Army Form C.2118

Hdqrs. 56 L N W R.E.

Place	Date 1917	Hour	Summary of Events and Information	Remarks and references to Appendices
LA GORGUE	3/2		C.R.E. left for England on leave	
"	4/2		Major F.G.P. GEDGE arrived to act	
"	5/2		Visited front line.	
"	6/2		Visited front line	
"	7/2		Visited front line.	
"	8/2		Visited front line.	
"	11/2		Visited front line	
"	12/2		Visited front line	
"	14/2		Visited front line	
"	15/2		Visited front line.	
"	17/2		Visited front line	
"	18/2		Visited front line	
"	21/2		Visited front line	
"	22/2		Visited front line. Received 56 L/Fld Order No 69.	
			C.R.E. returned from leave.	

SECRET.   Copy No. 4.

R.E. Operation Order No. 80.

Warning Order.
—*—*—*—*—*—*—

1. The 56th Division will shortly be relieved, the relieving will probably commence from the left on the 1/2nd March.

2. Further orders will be issued later.

3. ACKNOWLEDGE.

                                        J.G. Mudge
                                        Major R.E., A/C.R.E.,
23/2/17.   56th Division.

   Distribution.

        Copy Nos.   1. 512th London Fd.Co.R.E.
                    2. 513th London Fd.Co.R.E.
                    3. 416th Edinburgh Fd.Co.R.E.
                  ✓ 4. War Diary.
                    5. File.

SECRET.   Copy No. 6.

R.E.
56th Divnl. Order No.81.

Reference Trench Map RICHEBOURG 1/10,000.
"   Combined sheet BETHUNE   1/40,000.

~~23rd February, 1917.~~

Owing to a re-distribution of the Front between the 1st and XIth Corps, the boundary between the 56th and 5th Divisions will, on February 27th, be adjusted.

The new boundary will run from Canadian Orchard (S.22.c.45.00.) - S.27.a.60.35. - S.26.b.80.85. - S.25.b.70.35. - X.30.a.45.85.- X.21.a.20.40. - X.14.a.20.20. - W.11.a.60.00. thence along NORTH BANK of CANAL to P.36.a.80.70.

2. By 6-0pm on the 27th February Brigade fronts will be adjusted as under:-

RIGHT BRIGADE. S.22.c.45.00. to CHURCH ROAD (S.5.a.90.20.) inclusive.

CENTRE BRIGADE. CHURCH ROAD (S.5.a.90.20.) exclusive to WINCHESTER STREET (M.30.a.40.90.) inclusive.

LEFT BRIGADE. WINCHESTER STREET (M.30.a.40.90.) exclusive to BOND STREET (N.8.d.90.00.)

3. The following will be the boundaries between

(a)   RIGHT & CENTRE BRIGADES.

S.5.a.90.20. - CHURCH ROAD - (exclusive to Centre Brigade) - L.& N.W.Rly. (inclusive to Centre Brigade) - M.26.a.80.70. - M.19.d.90.80. - M.23.b.80.20.

(b)   CENTRE & LEFT BRIGADES.

M.30.a.40.90. - WINCHESTER STREET (exclusive to Left Brigade) S.E.Rly. - EPINETTE DUMP (common to both Brigades) - M.16.a.60.50. - M.10.d.00.00. - M.10.a.10.50. - M.4.c.80.70. - M.1.d.20.50.

4. The boundaries between Field Company Sectors will be similar to that of Brigades.

    513th London Field Company R.E. - Right Brigade Sector.
    416th Edinburgh Fd. Company R.E.- Centre   do   do
    512th London Field Company R.E. - Left   do   do

5. D.T.O. and D.D.O. will arrange to take over from the 5th Division Tramways and Drains, respectively.

6. Company H.Q. will remain as at present.

7. ACKNOWLEDGE.

                                            Capt. & Adjt. R.E.
                                            G.R.E., 56th Division
                                            For C.R.E. 56th DIVL ENGRS

24/2/17.
    Copy Nos. 1. 512th Field Co.
               2. 513th Field Co.   5. D.D.O.
               3. 416th Field Co.   6. War Diary.
               4. D.T.O.   7. File.

SECRET.   Copy No. 4

56th DIVISIONAL ENGINEERS ORDER No 82.

27th February 1917.

1.   The Division will be relieved in the line by the 49th Division, and will be gradually transferred to the Third Army, where it will be administered by the XIX Corps.

2.   It will move as shown in the attached March Tables.

3.   Supply railheads will be notified later.

4.   All reliefs will be arranged by Brigadier-Generals Commanding direct.

5.   C.R.E's will arrange for the relief of Head Qrs. R.E. Workshops, etc. The Field Companies will be relieved under orders of the Brigadier-Generals Commanding in whose sectors they are working.

6.   All defence schemes, sector maps, trench stores and aeroplane photos will be handed over and receipts taken.

7.   The Command of the Left Sector of the XIth Corps Front will pass to the G.O.C., 49th Division on completion of relief.

8.   ACKNOWLEDGE.

                                              Captain & Adjt R.E.
                                           for C.R.E. 56th Division.

Copy No. to

1. 416th Edinburgh Field Coy R.E.
2. 512th London Field Coy R.E.
3. 513th London Field Coy R.E.
4. War Diary.
5. File.

Serial No.	Date 1917.	Unit	From	To	Route	Remarks.
6.	Mch 1/2nd	169th Inf.Bde. Group.	Line; Left Section.	LA GORGUE-LESTREM BOUT DEVILLE- VIEILLE CHAPELLE.		On relief by 146th Infantry Bde. Group.
	Mch 2nd	do.	LA GORGUE-LESTREM- BOUT DEVILLE- VIEILLE CHAPELLE. XX ST.VENANT AREA.	ST.VENANT AREA.	No restrictions, under orders of the B.G.C. 169th Inf.Bde.	Units of Bde Group will march at interval of 500 yards between Units. Not to enter LILLERS before 12 noon.
	Mch 3rd	do.		PERNES AREA.		
	Mch 4th	do.	PERNES AREA.	WILLEMAN No. 1 AREA.		
	Mch 5th	do.	WILLEMAN No. 1 AREA.	WILLEMAN No. 3 AREA.		
7.	Mch 4th	1/5th Ches. Regt.	Laventie.	MERVILLE- HAZEBROUCK RD. K.21. & K.22.		To be clear of LAVENTIE by 12noon.
			By bus to THIRD ARMY.			
8.	Mch 5/6th	167th Inf.Bde. Group.	Line- Centre Section.	LA GORGUE-LESTREM -BOUT DEVILLE- VIEILLE CHAPELLE.		On relief by 148th Inf. Bde. Group.
9.	Mch 6th.	56th Division (less 168th & 169th Inf. Bde Groups & Divl Arty.)	LA GORGUE-LESTREM -BOUT DEVILLE- VIEILLE CHAPELLE.	ST.VENANT AREA.	No restrictions under orders of the B.G.C. 168th Inf.Bde.	Units of Brigade Group will march at intervals of 500 yds between Units.
	7th	do	ST.VENANT AREA.	PERNES AREA		
	8th	do	PERNES AREA.	WILLEMAN No. 2 XXX AREA.		

Serial No.	Date.	Unit.	From	To.	Route	Remarks.
		Artillery				
10.	Mch 8/9th					On relief by 147th Inf.Bde Group.
11.	Mch 9/10th	168th Inf.Bde. Group plus Medium T.Ms except actual Mortars & technical stores belonging to Mortars.	Line,Right Section.	LA GORGUE-LESTREM -BOUT DEVILLE- VIEILLE CHAPELLE. etc.		
	Mch 10th or 11th		FIRST ARMY AREA.	THIRD ARMY AREA.		If by Tactical Train on March 10th, if by Road on March 11th Group will be accomodated in WILLEMAN-AREA-NO-I. Further orders will be issued.

WAR DIARY
INTELLIGENCE SUMMARY

Army Form C. 2118.

Hdqrs. 56th Div. R.E.

Vol. 14

Place	Date	Hour	Summary of Events and Information	Remarks and references to Appendices
LA GORGUE	1911 March 1		Visited front line	
"	2		Visited front line with C.R.E. 49th Div.	
"	3		C.E. XI Corps called re the division leaving the Corps.	
"	4		Received 56th Divisional Order No. 70	
"	5		Completed the handing over to C.R.E. 49th Div.	
"	6		Office staff moved by motor lorry to HILLEMAN, the transport going by road to ST VENANT	
HILLEMAN	7		Transport continued the march as far as ST POL. Received 56th Divisional Order No. 71	
LE CAUROY	8		Transport continued to LE CAUROY. The office staff moved by motor lorry arriving at LE CAUROY at 6 p.m. Received 56th Div Order No. 72	
"	9		Visited the various Corps Parks	
"	10		Visited ARRAS and ACHICOURT	
"	11		Attended Conference at Div. Hdqrs. afterwards visiting VII Corps Hdqrs. Received 56th Div Order No. 73	

WAR DIARY
INTELLIGENCE SUMMARY

Army Form C. 2118.

Place	Date	Hour	Summary of Events and Information	Remarks and references to Appendices
	1917 March			
LE CAUROY	12		Visited forward area with Adjt to select site for Divisional Dumps	
"	13		Received Amendment to 56th Div Order N° 73. Visited the C.R.E.s of the 14th & 30th Divisions	
			Adjutant went to BAVINCOURT to arrange for the taking over of by the 88th Aux¹ Workshops.	
			Issued Order N° 83. Copy attached	A
GOUY EN ARTOIS	14		Moved to GOUY EN ARTOIS by road. Visited C.E. VII Corps. Received 56th Div Instructions N° 1 giving details for the VII Corps offensive.	
			513th Field Coy moved into line, billets at ACHICOURT.	
"	15		Visited O.C. 181st Tunnelling Coy R.E. to find out what work they have in hand for this division. Adjt visited the Corps Parks	
"	16		Visited DAINVILLE with C.E. VII Corps to meet C.R.E. 14th Divn to discuss the Corps Boundary	
"	17		Visited forward area	

Army Form C. 2118.

WAR DIARY
or
INTELLIGENCE SUMMARY.
(Erase heading not required.)

Instructions regarding War Diaries and Intelligence Summaries are contained in F. S. Regs., Part II. and the Staff Manual respectively. Title pages will be prepared in manuscript.

Place	Date	Hour	Summary of Events and Information	Remarks and references to Appendices
	1917 March			
GOUY EN ARTOIS	18		Visited forward area. Received 56th Div Order No 74.	
"	19		The enemy evacuated BEAURAINS last night. Last night the road to BEAURAINS was cleared and 6 bridges erected. The road was clear by this morning. Visited forward area. Received 56th Div Order No 75	
			Moved by road to BEAUMETZ	
BEAUMETZ	20		Visited forward area.	
"	21		Visited forward area. O.C. 1/5th Cheshire Reg (Pioneers) called, or again coming under my orders, as to work in hand. The whole of the Regiment put on repairs to roads. Received orders from Div that the 11th & 512 Field Coys will move into the line under my orders	
			Issued Order No 84. Copy attached	B
"	22		Received 56th Div Order No 76. Issued Order No 85. Copy attached. Visited forward area.	C

Army Form C. 2118.

WAR DIARY
—OR—
INTELLIGENCE SUMMARY.
(Erase heading not required.)

Place	Date	Hour	Summary of Events and Information	Remarks and references to Appendices
	1917 March			
BEAUMETZ	23		Visited forward area. Received 5th Arm Order N° 77. Took over Corps from line from 1st Division.	
"	24		Visited forward area. Attended C.E. VII Corps to Confer about roads and carriage of R.E. Stores. The want of transport makes it impossible for me to keep the Companies supplied with R.E. material	
"	25		Visited forward area	
"	26		Visited forward area. Issued Order N° 86. Copy attached.	D
"	27		Visited forward area. Issued Amendment to Order N° 86. Copy attached.	D¹
"	28		Issued Order N° 87. Copy attached	E
"	29		Received orders from Chief Engineer that Light Ry should be extended on ACHICOURT to M.3.C.3.2.	
"	30		Visited forward area	

Army Form C. 2118.

WAR DIARY
INTELLIGENCE SUMMARY.
(Erase heading not required.)

Instructions regarding War Diaries and Intelligence Summaries are contained in F.S. Regs., Part II. and the Staff Manual respectively. Title pages will be prepared in manuscript.

Place	Date	Hour	Summary of Events and Information	Remarks and references to Appendices
BEAUMETZ	1917 March 3/		Visited forward area: Received S.O. 4th Nov Order No 78. Issued Order No 88. Copy attached. 21st & 28th Attached. Work Report for week ending.	F G & H

The scarcity of M. Transport has seriously interfered with the supply of tools & stores for the work in hand & the assembling of a reserve of stores for operations has been undertaken. The distance of the Corps & Army dumps & parks being so far to rear it is unfortunate to use M Transport & this is just obtainable.— No provision is made for carriage of RE stores and is time of stress the available lorries are all used for ammunition & supplies, & RE work consequently suffers. This is more of (parents) when (as in case of 57th Div.) no divisional dumps have been established in the divisional area and the division only takes over the area at the last moment.

J.S. [signature]

SECRET.   Copy No...5...

56th DIVISIONAL ENGINEERS ORDER No. 83.

1.   The 56th Division is to take over the Centre Section of the VIIth Corps front (M.10.c.2.2. - M.4.b.3.1.) on March 13th and 14th.

2.   The 169th Infantry Brigade will take over the above frontage as per relief table attached.

3.   The responsibility of the 169th Infantry Brigade for defence within its boundaries extends as far back as the N & S line through the centre of DAINVILLE.
        The boundaries of the Section are as follows:-

RIGHT BOUNDARY (with 30th Division.)
M.10.c.2.2. - M.9.b.20.05. - M.9.a.5.6. - thence ACHICOURT - AGNY Railway at M.3.c.5.5. - bridge M.2.d.7.2. - Track to M.2.c.9.4. - M.2.c.7.2. - thence GOWER STREET (inclusive)

LEFT BOUNDARY (with 14th Division.)
M.4.b.3.1. - Support Line at M.4.a.98.30. - Reserve Line at M.4.a.50.85. - G.33.d.95.40. - thence HAVANNAH STREET (inclusive).

4.   Billeting parties of L.R.B., Q.V.R., Q.W.R., and 513th Field Coy. R.E. will report to Town Majors of their respective areas on morning of their move.

5.   Transport Lines will be at SIMENCOURT.

6.   Completion of relief to be reported in "B.A.B." Code to this office.

7.   Brigade Headquarters will close at GOUY-en-ARTOIS at 6-0pm on 14th, and will open at same hour at DAINVILLE.

8.   ACKNOWLEDGE.

                                                    H.Henderson
                                                    Capt.R.E., & Adjt.,for
                                                    C.R.E., 56th Division.
13/3/17.

        Distribution:
            Copy No.   1. 416th (Edinburgh) Fd.Co.R.E.
                        2. 512th (London) Fd.Co.R.E.
                        3. 513th (London) Fd.Co.R.E.
                        4. Headquarters "G".
                        5. War Diary.
                        6. File.
                        7. 169th Infantry Brigade.

RELIEF & MARCH TABLE of 513th (London) Field Co. R.E.

Date March.	From.	To.	Starting Point and time.	Route.	Remarks.
14th.	OPPY	SIMENCOURT.	9-0am.	SOMBRIN - BARLY - FOSSEUX - WANQUETIN.	Billeting party to report to Town Major, SIMENCOURT.
15th.	SIMENCOURT	ACHICOURT.	Cross Roads in BEAUMETZ-les-LOGES on ARRAS-DOULLENS Rd. 6-0pm.		Billeting party to report to Town Major, ACHICOURT.

Steel helmets to be worn by all ranks.

Pontoons should be off-loaded at SIMENCOURT&

SECRET.   Copy No. 5

56th DIVISIONAL ENGINEERS ORDER NO. 54.

1.   The 512th (London) Field Company R.E. will move to-morrow, (22nd inst.) afternoon from BARENCOURT to AGNY, making use of the direct BAINVILLE-ACHICOURT road.

2.   Billeting party to report to Town Major, AGNY in the morning of 22nd inst. to take over billets and select wagon lines.

3.   The party at BARENCOURT will rejoin the company after completion of work.

4.   ACKNOWLEDGE.

                                                      Lieut. Col. R.E.
21/5/17.   C.R.E., 56th Division.

Copy No.   1.   512th (London) Field Coy R.E.
           2.   Headquarters "G".
           3.   "   "Q".
           4.   56th Divisional Train.
           5.   War Diary.
           6.   File.

SECRET.   Copy No. 5.

56th. DIVISIONAL ENGINEERS ORDER NO. 85.

1.   The 416th. (Edinburgh) Fd. Coy. R.E. (less two sections) and the 193rd. (Div) S.S.Coy. will move from SIMENCOURT to MONCHIET on the 23rd. inst.

2.   The two Officers Commanding will mutually arrange the hour of move.

3.   Billeting Party will report to Town Major, MONCHIET.

4.   ACKNOWLEDGE.

N.

Issued at 8-30 a.m.   Capt. & Adjt. R.E.,
22/8/17.   for C.R.E., 56th. Division.

Copy No. 1. 416th. (Edinburgh) Field Co. R.E.
        2. Headquarters "A"
        3.   "   "B"
        4. 56th. Divisional Train.
        5. War Diary.
        6. File.

SECRET.   Copy No......

56th DIVISIONAL ENGINEERS ORDER No. 56.

1. The section of the 416th (Edinburgh) Field Coy R.E. now at RUBBERCOURT will move to MONCHIET to-morrow, 27th inst.

2. Two sections of the 416th (Edinburgh) Field Coy R.E. will move to Elephant shelters in G.35.c.8.4. on 28th inst.

3. An officer will see Town Major, ASHICOURT to obtain billets for transport.

4. Route via WAILLY.

5. No restrictions as to time.

6. ACKNOWLEDGE.

Issued at 6-30 pm   Capt. & Adjt. R.E.
26/4/17.   for C.R.E., 56th Division.

Copy No. 1. 416th (Edinburgh) Field Coy R.E.
        2. Headquarters "A"
        3.   "   "Q"
        4. 56th Divisional Train.
        5. War Diary.
        6. File.

SECRET.   Copy No. 5

Amendment to

56th DIVISIONAL ENGINEERS ORDER No. 86.

Paragraph 2 of the above order should read

"The 416th (Edinburgh) Field Coy R.E., less two sections,
will move to Elephant Shelters at G.35.c.6.4. on 28th inst.

Issued at 7-50 pm   Capt. & Adjt. R.E.
27/5/17.   for C.R.E., 56th Division.

Copy No. 1. 416th (Edinburgh) Field Coy R.E.
         2. Headquarters "Q"
         3.   "   "G"
         4. 56th Divisional Train
         5. War Diary
         6. File

SECRET.   Copy No. 8

56th Divisional Engineers Order No. 87.

1. Two sections 416th (Edinburgh) Field Coy R.E. and two sections of 512th (London) Field Coy R.E. are alloted for work in the Brigade areas to be occupied by their Brigades to which they are respectively affiliated, i.e., 167th and 168th Brigades.

2. They will be employed in reclaiming dugouts, arranging for forward dumps of R.E. material and any other work in connection with the operations which they may be required to do by the Brigade Commanders.

3. O's. Commanding should get into touch with Brigade staffs in this connection.

4. The Trench pioneers of the 167th and 168th Brigades are in ACHICOURT and should work in with the R.E.

5. A map is attached showing Brigade areas.   *(To 416 & 512 Field Coys only.)*

6. Every opportunity must be taken by all Officers and N.C.Os. of reconnoitring the ground and making themselves thoroughly acquainted with the trenches and general lie of the land.

Issued at 11-30 am
28/3/17.

                                              Lieut. Col. R.E.
                                              C.R.E., 56th Division.

Copy No. 1. 416th (Edinburgh) Field Coy R.E.
        2. 512th (London) Field Coy R.E.
        3. 513th (London) Field Coy R.E.
        4. 167th Infantry Brigade.
        5. 168th Infantry Brigade.
        6. 169th Infantry Brigade.
        7. "G"
        8. War Diary.
        9. File.

SECRET.   *F*   Copy No... 9 ...

56th DIVISIONAL ENGINEERS *Order* No. 88.
----

1. Reference 56th Divisional Order No. 78, relief of 169th Brigade by 167th and 168th Brigades.

2. Two sections 416th (Edinburgh) Field Coy R.E. and two sections 513th (London) Field Coy R.E. will be at the disposal of G.O.C. 167th Brigade and the 512th (London) Field Coy R.E. will be at the disposal of G.O.C. 168th Brigade for work in Brigade areas.

3. The remaining two sections of the 513th (London) Field Coy R.E. will work under orders of C.R.E.

4. Any definite work which has been started by 512th or 513th Field Coy must be completed by them.

5. Each Field Coy will place one pontoon wagon at the disposal of 181 Tunnelling Coy to bring up mining stores. O.C. 181 Tunnelling Coy R.E. will inform O's.C. Coys where and when transport is required.

6. This order will remain in force until Z - 1 day, ~~when~~ *as to which* further instructions will be issued.

7. ACKNOWLEDGE.

Issued at 3-40 pm
31/3/17.

Lieut. Col. R.E.
C.R.E., 56th Division.

Copy No. 1. 416th (Edinburgh) Field Coy R.E.
        2. 512th (London) Field Coy R.E.
        3. 513th (London) Field Coy R.E.
        4. 167th Infantry Brigade.
        5. 168th Infantry Brigade.
        6. 169th Infantry Brigade.
        7. "G"
        8. 181 Tunnelling Coy R.E.
        9. War Diary.
      10. File.

WORK REPORT

for Week ending noon March 21st 1917.

Divl Hdqtrs, Simencourt. 4 Nissen Huts completed. Latrines and Cookhouses commenced. Entrance to field widened and graded.
Work discontinued on 19th inst.

T.M.Emplacements. The 513 Coy were employed on these until the enemy's retirement, when they were at once abandoned and work commenced on the roads.

Roads. ACHICOURT-BEAURAINS. This has been cleared and made passable for wheel traffic up to the X roads BEAURAINS, M 10 b 65.85. Shell holes filled in and part of the top mud cleared off down to the metal.
Six new bridges over trenches have been constructed and four old ones strengthened.

ARRAS-BUCQUOY. One bridge strengthened and road reconnoitred and estimate made of metal required for immediate repairs.

Artillery track in No Mans Land, South of ACHICOURT-BEAURAINS road. 350 yards pegged out and side drains dug for 150 yards. 60 feet Timber ramp up to ACHICOURT-BEAURAINS road constructed.
An Earth ramp has also been constructed on to No Mans Land north of the road to assist R.F.A. with new positions.

Water Supply. A thorough reconnaisance of BEAURAINS has been made and 20 wells discovered. The majority of these were dry or filled in.
Two wells were found at M 10 b 55.95 and M 10 d 85.95 estimated to be 100 feet deep and about 10 feet of water. Samples have been taken and sent to 169th Brigade to be forwarded to A.D.M.S.

Dugouts and Cellars. All of these which are accessable have been examined for mobile charges. Two were found and the leads cut and charges removed. A dump of german aerial darts and egg bombs was discovered north of the road.

Dressing Station, ACHICOURT. Holing through the cellars on the plan handed over by outgoing Field Coy was continued until the enemy retirement. The work is at present in abeyance.

416th Coy. 2 Sections have been employed in the R.E. Workshops, BAVINCOURT The remainder of the Company have been training.

512th Coy. Have been training.

WORKS REPORT
for
week ending noon 28/3/17.

ROADS. Achicourt-Beaurains. This road is in a condition to take double line of heavy traffic from Achicourt to cross roads M.4.c.1.7. From this point to third (exclusive) trench across road at M.4.c.7.4. good for one line of heavy traffic only, centre of road. From this point to Beaurains only light traffic may proceed.

Main Arras-Achicourt Road is clear for heavy traffic. Bridge over stream in Achicourt is now repaired, and is fit for heavy traffic, but should only be used on one side for two days, to enable cement to set.

Agny-Bucquoy Road is clear for heavy traffic. Double track through Agny village.

Achicourt-Wailly Road is clear for heavy traffic, double track, but is very narrow where trenches pass under the road.

Road from M.15.b.6.0. to Beaurains. The Pioneers have cleared 100 yds. from the Southern end and about 360 yds. from the Northern end in the village. The Sappers have also one section working at the cross roads at M.16.a.8.8.

Beaurains-Neuville Vitasse. Cleared and bridged for single traffic 130 yds. beyond Beaurains X roads, a further 240 yds. partly cleared. *but fit for single traffic (horse) right through village*

Beaurains-Mercatel. Cleared of wire for 750 yds. Passable for horse traffic for 550 yds.

Emergency Track. Drains cut and wire cleared through to Beaurains-Bucquoy road, ramp constructed and road marked with white posts
Sunken Rd BEAURAINS-MERCATEL Clear for horse traffic

DUGOUTS. 169th Bde. H.Q. Completing and enlarging chambers and quarters for personnel.

M.18.b.1.3. Reclaiming auxiliary entrance and construction of 2nd chamber.

M.16.b. Cut and cover with loopholes for Divl Observers

Dugouts at Beaurains. Two sections have commenced at approx. M.11.c.0.5. clearing accomodation for themselves first, so that they can stay there whilst clearing the remainder.

C.Ts. Preussen Weg.) Clearing debris of felled trees to enable deepening
Stresow Weg.) to be begun.

Posts. at M.24.b.4.4., M.24.b.5.7., M.18.d.6.3., M.18.d.7.8. have been wired as necessary, deepened and firestepped.

Dressing Stations. Achicourt. Will be completed by 6 pm 29th inst.
M.4.b.0.8. The R.E. work will be finished to-night, the balance of filling being done by R.A.M.C.
Maison Brulee. New work commenced to-day, carpentry only.

Baths. Achicourt. Will be finished to-night.

Tramways. A R.E. Officer with 300 men of the 1st East Yorks has completed a further 650 yds. since taking over.

Mines. 3 mines in Achicourt have been disconnected and removed.

Tracing of Trenches
Deodar Lane. Traversed trench from Beaurains-Neuville Vitasse road to bank in M.24.c.
Support trench to above. Traversed trench from M.18.d.3.5. to Sunken Road in M.24.c.

Nissen Huts. 4 have been erected at Beaumetz, Q.23.d.6.9. complete with shelves, partitions and stoves. Also one cookhouse and two latrines, also 50 yds. of trench boarding laid.

MONCHIET. 5 cookhouses have been roofed and sides covered with wire-
netting and felt.
3 sign boards made and painted.
Latrine seats made.
Pump repaired at well.

Laundry, 2 chlorinating tanks 20'x5'x3' excavated, also one
Humbercourt. settling tank 14'x 8'x 4'6". The timbering is being
repaired.

Cable Trench. 200 pioneers were employed on this for one day.

Army Form C. 2118.

WAR DIARY
or
INTELLIGENCE SUMMARY.
(Erase heading not required.)

Headquarters
56th Divisional R.E.

Apl 15

Place	Date	Hour	Summary of Events and Information	Remarks and references to Appendices
	1917			
BEAUMETZ	1/4		Visited ACHICOURT to see about bridge over River CRINCHON for tanks. Site very bad for bridging, ground very soft and no bottom. Telephoned C.E. VII Corps on subject.	
"	2/4		Arranged for forward dumps with field coys. Visited 167 & 168 Brigades re Beaurains and stores tracks forward to Sunken Road and over Mercatel Road. Were completed this night. Issued Orders 89 and 90. Copies attached.	A & B
"	3/4		Held conference of Os of C 2 Field Coys and 1/5th Cheshire Regt on forthcoming operations. Minutes attached.	C
"	4/4		Altered design for strengthening tank bridge. Issued Order No 91 Me Field. Inspected WAILLY — BAC DU NORD road, it is very bad. Met Field Engineer of the Corps, who is reporting to Chief Engineer on the subject. Received 5th Divl Order No 99. Issued Order No 92. Copy attached	C.A. D

WAR DIARY
INTELLIGENCE SUMMARY

Army Form C. 21[?]

Place	Date	Hour	Summary of Events and Information	Remarks and references to Appendices
	1917			
BEAUMETZ	5/4		Inspected tank bridge. Visited Field Coy. Received S.B. & W.E. Order No. 80.	
"	6/4		Visited 512 & 513 Field Coys. Inspected WAILLY - BAC du NORD Road. Still very bad. 4 Tanks went over the bridge last night before the strengthening was completed, but no harm was done.	
"	7/4		Took 1/5 Cheshires off dugouts and put them on repairs to BEAURAINS Road. Hour 512 & 513 Field Coys. Issued Order No. 93. Copy attached.	E
"	8/4		ACHICOURT was bombarded this afternoon. 17 Ammunition lorries blowing up. Completely blocking the square.	2nd Lieut HASCOTT 32 Field Coy Killed in action 3rd Wm Parks Wounded in action
"	9/4		513 Field Coy and attached Infantry commenced clearing ACHICOURT Square at midnight last night. This enabled traffic to proceed early this morning. C.R.E. moved to Advanced Headquarters at 6 am this morning.	

WAR DIARY
INTELLIGENCE SUMMARY

Army Form C. 2118

Place	Date	Hour	Summary of Events and Information	Remarks and references to Appendices
BEAUMETZ	1917 9/4		At 10.30 a.m. wired 1/5th Cheshires that roads leading to NEUVILLE VITASSE through BEAURAINS are to be clear of Heavy Artillery as soon as possible. Also wired them to have 1 Company to clear road through NEUVILLE VITASSE in HANCOURT direction at dawn tomorrow. At midday a mixed party of Sappers, Cheshires & French Pioneers were sent out to dig and wire 2 Strong Points for 25 men each, N. of NEUVILLE VITASSE. These were completed and garrisoned in 4 hours. A larger party went out E. of NEUVILLE VITASSE to establish 3 Strong Points for 35 men each. These were completed in 6 hours. A Field Telegraph Heel Hatches were Consolidated in Conjunction with the London Scottish. 1/5 section also avoided 3 of Jordans and 1/4 Middlesex in Consolidating and wiring the Blue Line. 2 Lewis Gun Posts were made at the eastern side of NEUVILLE VITASSE	

WAR DIARY or INTELLIGENCE SUMMARY

Army Form C. 21

Place	Date	Hour	Summary of Events and Information	Remarks and references to Appendices
BEAUMETZ	1917 9/4		Parties were employed in searching for wells, dugouts & tunnels in NEUVILLE VITASSE. There appear to be plenty of dugouts but they will require considerable cleaning before occupation. Wells were found and samples of water sent for testing. 5 of them had been contaminated by the enemy with cow dung and some manure &c. The railway track between BEAURAINS & NEUVILLE VITASSE was reconnoitred with Chief Engineer X Corps Artillery, who are able to use the road towards NEUVILLE VITASSE through BEAURAINS.	
"	10/4		R.E dump established in BEAURAINS. 6 dugouts in NEUVILLE VITASSE have been searched and are ready for occupation, providing accommodation for 142 men. Forward dump established in NEUVILLE VITASSE. The BEAURAINS - MERCATEL road has been got clear for heavy traffic throughout the whole area.	

Army Form C. 2118

WAR DIARY
INTELLIGENCE SUMMARY.
(Erase heading not required.)

Instructions regarding War Diaries and Intelligence Summaries are contained in F. S. Regs., Part II. and the Staff Manual respectively. Title pages will be prepared in manuscript.

Place	Date	Hour	Summary of Events and Information	Remarks and references to Appendices
	1917			
BEAUMETZ	11/4		Visited NEUVILLE VITASSE. A German electric light plant had been found in NEUVILLE VITASSE and orders given for it to be repaired & set up.	
"	12/4		Moved by road to billets in ACHICOURT. Visited MANCOURT. Received 56th Div. Order No. 81.	
ACHICOURT	13/4		A reconnaissance of NEUVILLE VITASSE – ST MARTIN SUR COJEUR road has been made 1/5th "Cheshires" moved to dugouts between NEUVILLE VITASSE & BEAURAINS. Received 56th Div. Order No. 82.	
"	14/4		6 Craters & a number of shell holes were filled in, finished off with a good camber on the NEUVILLE VITASSE – HENIN road. Fair weather track constructed along the NEUVILLE VITASSE – ST MARTIN road. ST MARTIN – HENINEL road reconnoitred. 4 Wells in HENINEL examined, samples of water sent for testing. 3 of these were fit for drinking. Roads between NEUVILLE VITASSE, MANCOURT and ST MARTIN were inspected and reported on.	
"	15/4			

WAR DIARY
INTELLIGENCE SUMMARY
(Erase heading not required.)

Army Form C. 2118

Place	Date	Hour	Summary of Events and Information	Remarks and references to Appendices
ACHICOURT	1917 15/4		Another 2 wells discovered in NEUVILLE VITASSE & samples of water sent for testing, found fit for drinking. 15 dugouts have been opened up in NEUVILLE VITASSE, providing accommodation for 18 Officers & 353 O.Ranks. R.E. dump of material found in HENIN – containing 760 sacks cement, 400 Mining cases, 1000 Corr. Barbed wire, 5000 screw Pickets &c.	
"	16/4		Road from HENIN to HENINEL both sides of the River, have been inspected and reported on to-day. Temporary bridge erected at N.33.c.3.9. A bridge for heavy guns has been completed at N.20.a.3.5. Dugouts have been reclaimed at N.27.d. A large Crater cleared of earth & filled in with concrete slab and road material on MERCATEL – NEUVILLE VITASSE road.	
"	17/4		Repairs continued on the MERCATEL – BEAURAINS road. Received 7th Div. Order No. 83.	

WAR DIARY
INTELLIGENCE SUMMARY
(Erase heading not required.)

Army Form C.21

Place	Date	Hour	Summary of Events and Information	Remarks and references to Appendices
	1917			
ACHICOURT	17/4		Infantry tracks from NEUVILLE VITASSE to Kennel continued. Two bridges over River COJEUL completed. Received "B" and "C" Serg" H.INNS, 513 Gordon Field Co. R.E. for work on clearing roads and debris during bombardment on night of 8th inst. at ACHICOURT.	
"	18/4		Received 56th Auxil Bridge N° 84. 416 field Coy. 1 Other rank wounded. Issued Bridge N° 94. Copy attached.	F
"	19/4		Moved by road to COLIN for rest and training.	
COLIN	20/4		Issued Instructions to the Coy as to training whilst in the present area.	
"	21/4		Forwarded report on the work done by the No. 2 Engineers & Pioneers during operations E. of Arras 9/4/17 incl. to No. 2 Hd Qrs and to Chief Engineer VII Corps. Copy attached.	G
"	25/4		Moved by road to billets in HAUTEVILLE.	
HAUTEVILLE	26/4		Moved by road to billets in WARLUS. Received 56th Auxil Bridge N° 85.	

Army Form C. 2118

WAR DIARY
—or—
INTELLIGENCE SUMMARY.
(Erase heading not required.)

Instructions regarding War Diaries and Intelligence Summaries are contained in F. S. Regs., Part II. and the Staff Manual respectively. Title pages will be prepared in manuscript.

Place	Date 1917	Hour	Summary of Events and Information	Remarks and references to Appendices
WARLUS	27/4		Issued Order No. 95 Copy attached. CRE visited CRE 15th Divn as to the taking over from them down afterwards going over part of the line with him	H
"	28/4		Chief Engineer VI Corps came to give an outline of work required. Issued Order No. 96 Copy attached. CRE visited ARRAS	I
"	29/4		Moved by road to Hotel in ARRAS. Received 2nd Army Harvey Order No. 27 as to coming operations.	512 Coy 2 other ranks wounded
ARRAS	30/4		Visited forward area. Received 2nd Army Order No. 88. Issued Order No. 97 Copy attached. 116 Field Coy 1 other Rank wounded.	J

Jn Fenton
Lt. Col. R.E.
C.R.E. 56th Div. Engs.

T.134. Wt. W708—776. 500000. 4/15. Sir J. C. & S.

SECRET.   Copy No ...7....

56th. DIVISIONAL ENGINEERS' ORDER No. 89.

1. In the event of an advance special parties must be detailed to search for wells, and any other available water supply.

2. In the event of any wells being discovered, they must be at once reported to O.C., who will immediately take steps to have them labelled "not to be used for drinking purposes by troops". These labels are not to be removed until the water has been tested and reported on as "fit for drinking" by a competent Medical authority.

3. In every case, samples (not less than two quarts) will be taken by the R.E. in petrol tins provided for the purpose. These tins will be labelled with the Map reference of well from which sample was taken.

4. They will be sent to the nearest "Advanced Dressing Station" with a request that they be forwarded at once to D.H.Q. (Divisional Headquarters).

Issued at 8-30 a.m.
8/4/17.
                                                    Lt. Col. R.E.,
                                                    C.R.E., 56th. Division.

Copy No.1 to 416th (Edinburgh) Fd. Co. R.E.
       2.   512th. (London) Fd. Co. R.E.
       3.   513th. (London) Fd. Co. R.E.
       4.   A.D.M.S.
       5.   G.S.
       6.   A.Q.
       7.   War Diary.
       8.   File.

SECRET.   Copy No...6...

56th DIVISIONAL ENGINEERS ORDER No. 90.

1. The enemy's main defensive line runs as shown by the red line on the attached map, continuing South Eastwards along the COJEUL SWITCH.

2. The VII Corps attack is to be made on the frontage shown

   The 30th Division on the Right
   The 56th Division on the Centre
   The 14th Division on the Left.

3. The task of the 56th Division will be :-

   (a) 1st Objective.- The Capture of the blue line.
   (b) 2nd Objective.- The Capture of the portion of the COJEUL SWITCH situated within the Divisional Boundaries and the establishment of a line, approximately, as shown by the Brown line.

4. The attack is being carried out by the 167th Brigade on the right, and by the 168th Brigade on the left.
169th Brigade is in Divisional Reserve.

5. The objectives of 167th and 168th Brigades, and the dividing line between them is shown on the attached map.

6. Head Qtrs. and 2 sections of 416th (Edinburgh) Field Coy R.E. will be attached to 167th Infantry Brigade, and Head Qtrs. and 2 sections of 512th (London) Field Coy R.E. will be attached to 168th Infantry Brigade. One Company of 1/5th Cheshire Regt. will be attached to 168th Infantry Brigade.
2 sections of 416th (Ediburgh) Field Coy R.E., 2 sections of 512th (London) Field Coy R.E., 513th (London) Field Coy R.E. and 1/5th Cheshire Regiment (less one Company) will be in Divisional Reserve.

7. The probable programme of attack is as follows :-

   At Zero. VI Corps to assault, so as to bring it level with left of VII Corps.

   At Zero, plus 2 hours. 14th and 56th Divisions to assault and capture the blue line.

   At Zero, plus 6 hours, 40 minutes. 30th, 56th and 14th Divisions to assault and advance to the Brown line.

   N.B. The above programme is liable to modification.

8. Four tanks will probably be alloted to the 56th Division.

9. The assembly area for Z day for units in Divisional reserve is shown on attached map.

10. Divisional Headquarters will be at dugouts, at M.3.c.5.2.

11. Divisional Reserve will be held in readiness to move forward from Zero, plus 2 hours on Z day.

12. All Officers will set their watches by divisional signal time every day from now on.

13. ACKNOWLEDGE.

Issued at 5-0 pm
   2/4/17.
                                                  Lieut. Col. R.E.
                                                  C.R.E. 56th Division.

Copy No. 1. 416th (Edinburgh) Field Coy R.E.
2. 512th (London) Field Coy R.E.
3. 513th (London) Field Coy R.E.
4. 1/5th Cheshire Regiment.
5. "G"
6. War Diary.
7. File.

NOTES on Conference of O's. C. 3/4/17.

1. The situation was discussed generally and attention drawn to the following points :-

   1. **Information.** This is one of the primary points and it is essential that information, to be of value, must be rendered quickly and in a clear form.
   Information is required
      (a) As to position where R.E. work is required and is possible, giving essential stores and numbers required.
      (b) As to any work which is being undertaken by forward sections. If this information is known at Headquarters, there is much less chance of party suffering casualties from our own artillery.
      (c) As to any dumps of R.E. material discovered, giving location and contents.
      (d) As to any craters or demolished bridges on roads, giving nature of bridge, gap to be repaired and probable requirements in stores.
      (e) As to any dugouts discovered in order that arrangements may be made to reclaim.
      (f) As to wells and water supply generally.
   All the above should be reported on at once, and in addition a progress report should reach Headquarters at 8 a.m. daily.

   2. **Strong Points.**
   One section and 25 Infantry can construct a strong point for 20 men and 2 M.G's in about 6 hours.
   A type of cruciform strong point is issued herewith.
   In general do not site near sunken roads, cross roads or enemy dugouts. These will all be registered by enemy artillery.
   Arrangements should be made with Headquarters of Brigades for garrison of strong points to be available as soon as point is ready for occupation.

   3. **Communication Trenches.**
   Of zig-zag trace with rounded corners, the inclination of legs should be 3/1 to general direction.
   Profile 6' deep, 3' wide at bottom, 5'6" to 6' wide at top with a 2' berm.
   Do not site alongside road, as this tends to destroy road, and road is sure to be registered by enemy artillery.

   4. **Tracks** will be required for infantry and pack transport, these should be 6' wide and have a shallow trench on either side, in addition to pickets, in order to help keeping directions at night.
   Where possible tracks for pack transport and infantry should be made to relieve traffic on main roads.

   5. Special instructions have been issued as regards water.

   6. It is important that reconnaissance of any work to be done should be carried out, whenever possible, by daylight.
   The Officer making the reconnaissance should be accompanied by a N.C.O. and 2 runners in case of casualties, and also in order that guides to work, who know the route may be available.

   7. Any orderlies furnished must know their way to all dumps and R.E. Units as well as Bde. Headquarters.

   Generally. Endeavour to assist the operations by every means.
   Do not worry the Staff, but be on the spot and keep your ears open. The Staff will be very busy and will not encourage ~~irrelevant~~ conversation, but if an opportunity occurs of helping
   Irrelevant

it is our business to seize it.
　　In case of orders from Staff be sure that the orders are thoroughly understood, not only in the letter but in the spirit, and act accordingly.

[signature]

Lieut. Col. R.E.
C.R.E., 56th Division.

4/4/17.

Copy No. 1. 416th (Edinburgh) Field Coy R.E.
　　　　　2. 512th (London) Field Coy R.E.
　　　　　3. 513th (London) Field Coy R.E.
　　　　　4. 1/5th Cheshire Regiment.
　　　　　5. "G"
　　　　　6. War Diary.
　　　　　7. File.
　　　　　8 9 & 10. Spare.

SECRET.   Copy No. 5

56th DIVISIONAL ENGINEERS ORDER No. 91.

1. O.C. 512th (London) Field Coy R.E. will detail an Officer, 2nd Lieut. Robinson is suggested, to meet Lieut. Bell of "D" Battalion, 1st Brigade, Heavy Branch, M.G. Corps at 11 a.m. on 4th April at Divisional Headquarters.

2. This Officer will be prepared to be attached to "D" Battalion should his services be required.

3. 416th, 512th and 513th Field Companies will each detail a N.C.O. to report to the Officer selected by O.C. 512th Field Coy, should their services be required.

Issued at 3-15 p.m.
3/4/17.

Captain & Adjt. R.E.
for C.R.E., 56th Division.

Copy No. 1. 416th (Edinburgh) Field Coy R.E.
         2. 512th (London) Field Coy R.E.
         3. 513th (London) Field Coy R.E.
         4. "G"
         5. War Diary.
         6. File.

SECRET.   Copy No...7....

56th DIVISIONAL ENGINEERS ORDER No. 92.

1. The two sections, 416th (Edinburgh) Field Coy R.E. now working at Divisional Workshops, BAVINCOURT will move to ACHICOURT on Z - 1 day.

    Arrangements must be made with Town Major, ACHICOURT for billets. The transport will park on the Coy transport lines.

2. Headquarters and the two sections of 416th (Edinburgh) Field Coy R.E. attached to 167th Infantry Brigade must be clear of the dugouts in ACHICOURT Station, G.35.c.6.2. by noon on Z - 2 day.

    Application for accommodation from then must be made to Headquarters, 167th Brigade.

Issued at 7-30 p.m.   Lieut. Col. R.E.
       4/4/17.   C.R.E., 56th Division.

Copy No. 1. 416th (Edinburgh) Field Coy R.E.
        2. 167th Infantry Brigade.
        3. Town Major, Achicourt.
        4. Lieut. D.E.Clerk.
        5. "G"
        6. "Q"
        7. War Diary.
        8. File.

SECRET.   Copy No...6...

56th DIVISIONAL ENGINEERS ORDER No. 93.

1. Each Field Coy and the Pioneers will provide two runners for duty during the operations.

    One of these will report at Advanced Divl. R.E. Hdqtrs at 6 p.m. Z - 1 day, the second need not report until 6 a.m. Z day. They will bring rations, and will be on duty until dismissed.

2. All units in Divisional Reserve must be in their assembly positions by 3 a.m. Z day.

3. Locations of all detachments, in addition to Hdqtrs, must be sent to Advanced Divl R.E. Hdqtrs, and any change will be notified at the earliest possible moment.

Issued at 9 a.m.   Lieut. Col. R.E.
7/4/17.   C.R.E., 56th Division.

Copy No. 1. 416th (Edinburgh) Field Coy R.E.
         2. 512th (London) Field Coy R.E.
         3. 513th (London) Field Coy R.E.
         4. 1/5th Cheshire Regiment.
         5. "Q"
         6. War Diary.
         7. File.

SECRET.   Copy No. 8

56th DIVISIONAL ENGINEERS ORDER No. 94.

1.   30th Division is to relieve 56th Division (less artillery).

2.   416th (Edinburgh) Field Coy R.E. will concentrate at ACHICOURT to-night and march to COUIN Area on 19th instant.

3.   512th (London) Field Coy R.E. will concentrate at AGNY on 19th and march to SOUASTRE Area on 20th instant.

4.   513th (London) Field Coy R.E. will concentrate at ACHICOURT on 19th and march to POMMIER Area on 20th instant.

5.   Field Companies R.E. will be located with their affiliated Infantry Brigades after relief, and the O's. C. Companies will get in touch with Brigades afterxrelief and arrange for billeting accommodation in their areas.

6.   Divisional Engineers H.Q. will close at its present location at 10 a.m. 19th instant, and will then open at COUIN.

7.   ACKNOWLEDGE.

Issued at 5-45 p.m.   Lieut. Col. R.E.
        18/4/17.   C.R.E., 56th Division.

Copy No. 1. 416th (Edinburgh) Field Coy R.E.
        2. 512th (London) Field Coy R.E.
        3. 513th (London) Field Coy R.E.
        4. 167th Infantry Brigade.
        5. 168th Infantry Brigade.
        6. 169th Infantry Brigade.
        7. "G"
        8. War Diary.
        9. File.
       10. "Q"

Distribution of, and work done by,
R.Es. and Pioneers
during the operations S.E. of ARRAS, April 1917.

1. Two sections of R.Es, and two platoons of Pioneers were attached to each of the two assaulting Brigades for work on forward tracks, construction of Strong Points and consolidation, etc. Brigade Trench Pioneers assisted the R.Es. and supplied the necessary carrying parties.

    Work Done.
    2 Strong Points for 25 men each were dug and wired in 4 hours, N.E. of NEUVILLE VITASSE.
    3 Strong Points for 35 men each were dug and wired in 6 hours, E. of NEUVILLE VITASSE.
    2 Strong Points were dug and wired S. of HENINEL.
    In conjunction with the Infantry, Card and Telegraph Hill Trenches and the whole of the Blue Line were consolidated.
    Consolidation was also carried out at WANCOURT TOWER after the counter attack.
    Lewis Gun Posts were made E. of NEUVILLE VITASSE.
    Forward Tracks were cleared for horse transport and artillery.

2. Two sections of R.Es. were employed on searching for Mines, clearing and repairing Wells and Dugouts in captured villages, and taking samples of water and labelling wells.

    Work Done.
    Dugouts. 15 were cleared and repaired in NEUVILLE VITASSE, providing accommodation for 18 Officers & 353 O.R.
    52 were cleared and repaired in BEAURAINS, providing accommodation for over 750 men.

    Wells. 8 were found in NEUVILLE VITASSE and samples of water sent for testing. 5 of these were found to have been contaminated by the enemy with horse manure, cow dung, etc.
    10 were found in HENINEL and samples sent for testing, 6 of these were fit for drinking.

    Mines. 2 mines were found, they were disconnected and the charges drawn.

3. One section of R.Es. was kept in reserve for work of immediate importance.

    Work Done.
    This section did useful work in keeping the traffic going at night, by filling in ruts and making small diversions where necessary.

4. The remainder of the R.Es. and Pioneers were employed on clearing, repairing and maintaining roads, constructing and strengthening bridges, and making fair weather tracks.

    Work Done.
    Bridges. A bridge over the River Crinchon was strengthened to take tanks, in 48 hours. A blue print of the work done is attached.
    3 bridges were constructed over the River Cojeul to take heavy artillery, in 12 hours.
    2 trenches were bridged E. of NEUVILLE VITASSE to take horse transport and field guns.

    Roads. 4250 yards Fair Weather Track was made.
    26000 yards of road was cleared and repaired for horse transport.
    18000 yards of road was repaired and made good for motor lorry traffic.

Roads.   After the bombardment of ACHICOURT, R.Es., in conjunction
(contd) with Pioneers, cleared the roads round the square in
5 hours, to enable traffic to proceed through village.

5.   In addition to the above, R.E. Officers were engaged in reconnaissance of roads, tramways and R.E. stores in the captured area.

6.   Owing to the difficulty in obtaining mechanical transport, the transport of the Companies was pooled, and put under an Officer, who was made responsible for getting up R.E. material.

    This was found to be quite inadequate, and it was not until lorries were provided that a sufficient quantity of stores could be got forward.

Lieut. Col. R.E.
C.R.E., 56th Division.

21/4/17.

SECRET.   Copy No... 8

56th DIVISIONAL ENGINEERS ORDER No. 95.

1. 56th Division is to relieve 15th Division in the Line and has now come under the orders of VI Corps.

2. 416th (Edinburgh) Field Coy R.E. will relieve 73rd Field Coy R.E. on the 28th inst.
    Headquarters and Horse Lines will be at G.23.c.5.1.

3. 512th (London) Field Coy R.E. will relieve 74th Field Coy R.E. on the 28th inst.
    Headquarters and Horse Lines will be at G.23.c.6.1.

4. 513th (London) Field Coy R.E. will relieve 91st Field Coy R.E. on the 28th inst.
    Headquarters will be at G.27.b.8.8., but as the 91st Coy have had Mange in their stables, an Officer will have to be detailed to find convenient Horse Lines.

5. The three Companies will be clear of their present billets by 10 a.m.

6. 1/5th Cheshire Regiment will relieve the Pioneer Battn of the 15th Division on the 28th inst.
    Headquarters will be at Rue de Rapporteurs, off Theatre Place, G.22.d.1.7. Horse Lines will be at DUISANS.
    No restrictions as to time or route.

7. ACKNOWLEDGE.

Issued at 3-30 p.m.   Capt. & Adjt. R.E.
       27/4/17.   for C.R.E., 56th Division.

Copy No. 1. 416th (Edinburgh) Field Coy R.E.
         2. 512th (London) Field Coy R.E.
         3. 513th (London) Field Coy R.E.
         4. 1/5th Cheshire Regiment.
         5. "G"
         6. "Q"
         7. 56th Divisional Train.
         8. War Diary.
         9. File.

SECRET.   Copy No. 4

              56th DIVISIONAL ENGINEERS ORDER No. 96.
              ═══════════════════════════════════════

1.   Two sections of 416th (Edinburgh) Field Coy R.E. will
    come under orders of G.O.C. 167th Infantry Brigade at 4 p.m.
    to-morrow, 29th instant.

2.   The O.C. Coy will get in touch with Brigade before
    that time to receive instructions.

                                              Lieut. Col. R.E.
Issued at 5 p.m.   C.R.E., 56th Division.
    28/4/17.

Copy No. 1. 416th (Edinburgh) Field Coy R.E.
         2. 167th Infantry Brigade.
         3. "Q"
         4. War Diary.
         5. File.

SECRET.   Copy No. 5

56th Divisional Engineers Order No. 97.

1. The Fifth, Third and First Armies are to attack simultaneously on "Z" day, the main objective being a line FONTAINE LES CROISILLES-CHERISY-ST ROHART FACTORY-BOIS DU VERT-BOIS DU SART-PLOUVAIN Station-SQUARE WOOD (C.27.c.)

2. The object of the VI Corps is to capture and consolidate the RED LINE as shown on the attached map "B".

3. The 3rd Division will be on the left of 56th Division.
   The 14th Division (VII Corps) will be on the right.

4. The objective of 56th Division is the RED LINE within the Divisional Boundaries.

5. The attack will be carried out by 169th Infantry Brigade on the right, and by 167th Infantry Brigade on the left.
   The dividing line between Brigades and the areas allotted for their assembly are shown on the attached map "B".
   The magnetic bearing of the dividing line is approximately 103 degrees.

6. As soon as the RED LINE is captured it will be consolidated and patrols, supported by formed bodies of Infantry, will be pushed forward in order to gain ground towards the GREEN LINE *dotted* shown on the attached map.
   The first objective of these patrols will be an approximate line O.10.b.90.- RIVER - PONT A TROIS GUEULES.
   According as the troops on our right and left progress and make good VIS EN ARTOIS AND THE HIGH ground about BOIRY NOTRE DAME, these patrols will push further forward to approximately the line O.11.a.40. - bridge O.11.c.54. - the Sunken Road O.17.a. & c.
   These patrols must be supplied with means of Visual communications.

7. 167th and 169th Infantry Brigades will be closed up into their concentration areas East of, and including the WANCOURT LINE by 11 p.m. on "Y" day.

8. 168th Infantry Brigade will be clear of ARRAS by 8 p.m. on "Y" day.
   H.Q. will be established at H.31.central. and units will be accommodated between the WANCOURT LINE (exclusive) and the old German front line (inclusive) within the Divisional boundaries, with the two leading Battalions about N.2.c. and d.
   As and when G.Os.C. 167th and 169th Infantry Brigades move forward their Reserve Battalions from the WANCOURT LINE, they will inform G.O.C. 168th Infantry Brigade, who will move up Battalions to take their place.

9. ~~G.O.C. 168th Infantry Brigade will arrange to carry out reconnaissances with a view to the advance of his Brigade to the dotted GREEN or GREEN LINES, should it be called upon.~~
   ~~As this advance might take place after dark all arrangements should be made accordingly and compass bearings taken.~~

10. The following R.E. and Pioneers will be allotted to 167th and 169th Infantry Brigades for the operations :-

    167th Infantry Brigade - 416th Field Coy R.E. (less 2 Sections)
                             1 Coy 5th Cheshire Regiment.

    169th Infantry Brigade - 2 Sections 416th Field Coy R.E.
                             1 Coy 5th Cheshire Regiment.

    Arrangements will be made by the C.R.E.

-2-

Arrangements will be made by the C.R.E. to attach two Sections of the 512th Field Coy R.E. and one Company Pioneers to 168th Infantry Brigade, in the event of the latter being ordered to carry on the advance beyond the RED LINE.

11.   "Z" day and Zero hour will be notified later.

12.   Divn H.Q. will remain at 15, Rue de la Paix, ARRAS.

13.   ACKNOWLEDGE.

Issued at 3-30 p.m.
 30/4/17.
                                        Lieut. Col. R.E.
                                   C.R.E., 56th Division.

Copy No. 1. 416th (Edinburgh) Field Coy R.E.
        2. 512th (London) Field Coy R.E.
        3. 513th (London) Field Coy R.E.
        4. "G"
        5. War Diary.
        6. File.

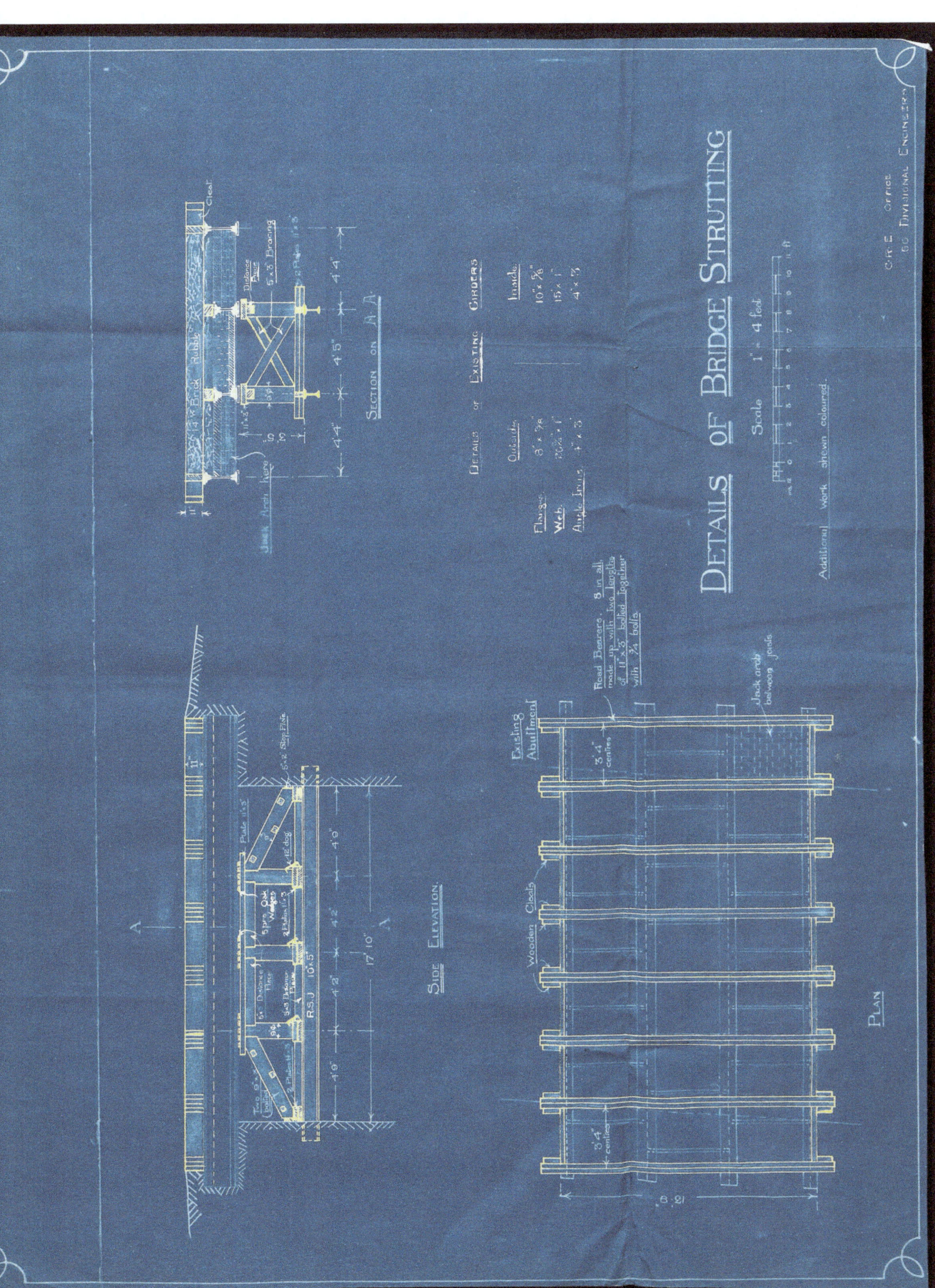

C.R.E.,
56th DIVISION.

No.
Date 4-5-17

Army Form C. 2118.

WAR DIARY
INTELLIGENCE SUMMARY
(Erase heading not required.)

Headquarters 56th Aust R.E.

Place	Date	Hour	Summary of Events and Information	Remarks and references to Appendices
ARRAS	1/5		C.R.E. visited forward area. Issued orders to 513 Coy that the 2 sections under 167th Bde will be withdrawn and put into Div Reserve to-morrow night. Casualties :- 416 Coy, 1 O.R. Killed, 3 O.R. Wounded, 1 O.R. Shell Shock. 513 Coy, 1 O.R. Wounded	
"	2/5		C.R.E. visited forward area. Issued orders 512 Coy (less 2 sections), 513 Coy and 2 Coys of 1/5 Cheshires to be in readiness to move forward. Casualties - 513 Coy, 2nd Lieut G. DYKE Wounded, 1 O.R. Killed. Casualties :- 513 Coy, 1 O.R. Wounded	
"	3/5		Received 56th Aust Order No 90.	
"	4/5		Issued orders that 2 sections 416 Coy and 2 sections 513 Coy now in the line will remain to work under 168th Bde. They will be relieved by 4 section 513 Coy to-morrow.	
"	5/5		Received 56th Aust Order No 91. Issued Order No 98. Copy attached	A

Army Form C. 2118

WAR DIARY
—of—
INTELLIGENCE SUMMARY.
(Erase heading not required.)

Instructions regarding War Diaries and Intelligence Summaries are contained in F.S. Regs., Part II. and the Staff Manual respectively. Title pages will be prepared in manuscript.

Place	Date 1917	Hour	Summary of Events and Information	Remarks and references to Appendices
ARRAS	5/5		Issued orders for 2 sections 513 Coy to reclaim and improve dugouts at H.31 central.	
"	6/5		Casualties:- 513 Coy. 2 O.R. wounded, at duty. C.R.E. visited forward area. Issued orders to 416 and 513 Coys to wire the WANCOURT line between No.6 central and ARRAS - CAMBRAI Road and to form pickets at suitable intervals.	
"	7/5		Casualties - 513 Coy. 2 O.R. killed, 10.R. wounded, 2.O.R. wounded, at duty. Issued orders for another Coy of 4/5th Cheshires to be put under 168th Bde.	
"	8/5		C.R.E. visited forward area. Issued orders to 416 and 513 Coys for the wiring of the WANCOURT line to be extended southwards to the TILLOY-WANCOURT line.	
"	9/5		C.R.E. visited forward area. Received 56th Div. Order No.92. Issued orders for 3 sections 513 Coy. to relieve 3 sections 416 Coy on the 10th	

Army Form C. 211

WAR DIARY
—or—
INTELLIGENCE SUMMARY.
(Erase heading not required.)

Place	Date 1917	Hour	Summary of Events and Information	Remarks and references to Appendices
ARRAS	10/5		C.R.E. and Adjutant, 37th Divn called as to the taking over by that Divn. Issued Order No 99. Copy attached. Issued orders to 1/5th Cheshires, 2 platoons to work on Nut Brake Trolley and 1 platoon o/c latrines &c for 169th Bde.	B
"	11/5		C.R.E. visited forward area. Received 56th Divn Order No 93. Issued orders for 1 section 512 Coy to relieve 1 section 473 Coy. Casualties :- 513 Coy :- 1 O.R. wounded.	
"	12/5		Casualties :- 512 Coy :- 2 O.R. wounded.	
"	13/5		Casualties :- 512 Coy :- 3 O.R. killed. 4 O.R. wounded. Sent in an application to Aut. Majors and asked that it may be forwarded, that Territorial R.E. Officers be allowed to wear the full R.E. badge.	
"	14/5		C.R.E. visited forward area. Casualties :- 512 Coy :- 1 O.R. wounded, at duty.	

Army Form C. 2118.

WAR DIARY
-or-
INTELLIGENCE SUMMARY.
(Erase heading not required.)

Instructions regarding War Diaries and Intelligence Summaries are contained in F.S. Regs., Part II. and the Staff Manual respectively. Title pages will be prepared in manuscript.

Place	Date	Hour	Summary of Events and Information	Remarks and references to Appendices
ARRAS	1917 15/5		C.R.E. worked forward area	
"	16/5		C.R.E. 37th Divn came to go into details of work in hand. Received 56th Divn Order No 94	
"	17/5		Casualties :- 416 Coy. 1 O.R. wounded, at duty. Signal Coy. 1 O.R. wounded. C.R.E. 37th Divn called. Received 56th Divn Orders 95, 96, 96a1, 96a2, and 97. Issued Order No 100. Copy attached. Casualties :- 512 Coy. 2 O.R. wounded, 513 Coy. 1 O.R. wounded.	C
"	18/5		C.R.E. visited forward area with C.R.E. 37th Divn. Received 56th Divn Order No 98. Issued orders - 416 Coy. to see 168th Bde after relief and to do what work is required. 513 Coy will take over on 21st the ranges at DUISANS and HABARCQ commenced by 416 Coy.	
"	20/5		Chief Engineer VII Corps came. Moved Hdy road to WARLUS.	
"	21/5		Issued orders to 416 Coy. to commence work on Officers Club, ARRAS	

Army Form C. 2118

WAR DIARY
INTELLIGENCE SUMMARY.
(Erase heading not required.)

Instructions regarding War Diaries and Intelligence Summaries are contained in F. S. Regs., Part II. and the Staff Manual respectively. Title pages will be prepared in manuscript.

Place	Date	Hour	Summary of Events and Information	Remarks and references to Appendices
	1917			
NARLUS	22/5		Received 5th Aust. Order No 99.	
			Issued Order No 101. Copy attached	D
	24/5		Moved by road to HABARCQ.	
			Instructions for training have been issued to the Cos.	
HABARCQ	25/5		Sections of the Cos. are working on Model trenches and	
"	26/5		strong points for the Infantry. Bayonet fighting Gallows	
"	27/5		are being constructed at GOUVES and MONTENESCOURT.	
"	28/5		C.R.E. attended G.O.C.'s conference at Aust. Hd/qrs.	
"	31/5		Issued Order No 102. Copy attached	E
			2 Cpls. 1/5th Cheshires have been sent to ARRAS to work under Chief Engineer, VI Corps.	

J. H. Forson
Lt. Col. R.E.
C.R.E. 66th DIV¹ ENG⁸

SECRET.   Copy No.....

56th Divisional Engineers Order No. 98.

1. The defensive boundary of the 56th Division is to be readjusted as follows :-

   Southern Boundary - The COJEUL RIVER.

   Northern Boundary with 3rd Division -

       Junction of HUSSAR & DRAGOON LANES -

       GRAPE Trench (inclusive to 3rd Division)

       Point O.8.a.85.90.

2. The readjustment will be made on night 6th/7th May under arrangements to be made direct between G.O.C. 168th Infantry Brigade & G.O.C. 8th Infantry Brigade (H.Q. N.5.a.8.8.), the former assuming command on conclusion of the relief.

3. ACKNOWLEDGE.

Issued at 7-45 p.m.   Lieut. Col. R.E.
5/5/17.   C.R.E., 56th Division.

Copy No. 1. 416th (Edinburgh) Field Coy R.E.
       2. 512th (London) Field Coy R.E.
       3. 513th (London) Field Coy R.E.
       4. War Diary.
       5. File.

SECRET.   Copy No........

50th DIVISIONAL ENGINEERS ORDER No. 99.

1. 150th Infantry Brigade will carry out an attack on the
    evening of 11th May, 1917, at an hour to be specified later,
    with the object of capturing :-

    (a) TOOL TRENCH from about C.8.b.11 to CAVALRY FARM.

    (b) CAVALRY FARM and

    (c) The trench S.E. of the Farm, which runs from about
        C.14.a.71 to C.14.b.58.

2. The objectives when gained will be consolidated at once
    and joined up with our present line, and a block will be established
    at the northern end of the captured portion of TOOL TRENCH.

3. The C.R.A. will arrange direct with O.C. 150th Infantry
    Brigade for the necessary Artillery preparation and barrages,
    including points it is desired to shell by Heavy Artillery.

4. VI Corps Heavy Artillery is to destroy the following trenches :-

    (a) TOOL TRENCH, North of C.8.b.33.34.

    (b) TOWN POLE TRENCH.

    (c) New communication trench between LANYARD TRENCH and
        TOOL TRENCH.

    Fire for destruction will be commenced on these trenches
    as soon as observation can be obtained on 10th May.

5. ACKNOWLEDGE.

Issued at 1 p.m.   Lieut. Col. R.E.
    10/5/17.   C.R.E., 50th Division.

Copy No. 1. 416th (Edinburgh) Field Coy. R.E.
        2. 512th (London) Field Coy. R.E.
        3. 513th (London) Field Coy. R.E.
        4. War Diary.
        5. File.

SECRET.   Copy No........

56th Divisional Engineers (Warning) Order No. 100.

1.   The 57th Division, less Artillery, is to relieve the 56th Division, less Artillery.

2.   ~~Reliefs will be effected by the Company and Companies on relief will be billeted with their normal brigade groups.~~

3.   The following will be the arrangements :-

   416th (Edinburgh) Field Coy R.E. will be relieved by 134th Field Coy R.E. on the 20th inst. and will march to BERNEVILLE. An advanced party of 134th Coy will arrive on the evening of 19th inst.

   512th (London) Field Coy R.E. will be relieved by 155th Field Coy R.E. on the 21st inst. and will march to WARLUS. An advanced party of 155th Coy will arrive on the 19th inst.

   513th (London) Field Coy R.E. will be relieved by 152th Field Coy R.E. on the 20th inst. and will march to DUISANS. An advanced party of 152th Coy will arrive on the evening of the 19th inst.

4.   No restrictions as to route, but each of the Companies will be clear of ARRAS by 10 a.m. on the dates given.

5.   General Officer Commanding 57th Division will assume command of the line at 10 a.m. on 21st May.

6.   Divisional Headquarters will close at ARRAS at 10 a.m. 21st May and will open at the same time probably at WARLUS.

7.   ACKNOWLEDGE.

Issued at 6-45 p.m.   Lieut. Col. R.E.
17/5/17.   C.R.E., 56th Division.

Copy No. 1. 416th (Edinburgh) Field Coy R.E.
         2. 512th (London) Field Coy R.E.
         3. 513th (London) Field Coy R.E.
         4. "Q"
         5. 56th Divisional Train.
         6. War Diary.
         7. File.

SECRET   Copy No......

56th DIVISIONAL ENGINEERS ORDER No. 101.

1. Moves will take place on the 24th as per attached March Table (Appendix "A")

2. Distribution of Units on completion of move is shown in Appendix "B".

3. A distance of 250 yards between Battalions and 100 yards between Companies and Regimental first line transport will be maintained.

4. Divl. H.Q. closes at WANLEU at 12 noon on the 24th May, and re-opens at the same hour at HABARCQ CHATEAU.

5. ACKNOWLEDGE.

Issued at 11-30 a.m.
22/5/17.

Lieut. Col. R.E.
C.R.E., 56th Division.

Copy No. 1. 416th (Edinburgh) Field Coy R.E.
        2. 512th (London) Field Coy R.E.
        3. 513th (London) Field Coy R.E.
        4. "Q"
        5. 56th Divisional Train.
        6. War Diary.
        7. File.

SECRET

ISSUED WITH 56th DIVISIONAL ENGINEERS ORDER No. 101.

APPENDIX "A"

Unit.	From	To	Route	Remarks.
416th Field Coy R.E.	BERNEVILLE	GOUVES	WARLUS	To be clear of WARLUS by 10 a.m.
512th Field Coy R.E.	WARLUS	SIMENCOURT	BERNEVILLE	Will fall in at the rear of 2do. (1) Not to enter SIMENCOURT before 11 a.m. (2) To be clear of BERNEVILLE by 12-15 p.m.
513th Field Coy R.E.	DUISANS	GOUVES	Direct	by brigade orders.

APPENDIX "B"

Area.	Troops to be accommodated	Area Commander	Billets allotted by
Part of GOUVES.	416th (Edin) Field Coy R.E.	O.C. 167th Inf. Bde.	Permanent Town Major.
Part of GOUVES	513th (London) Field Coy R.E.	O.C. 168th Inf. Bde.	" " "
SIMENCOURT.	512th (London) Field Coy R.E.	O.C. 169th Inf. Bde.	" " "

Area Commanders will arrange direct with Town Majors for the accommodation of the troops allotted to their Area.

SECRET.   Copy No.........

56th. DIVISIONAL ENGINEERS' ORDER No. 102.

1.   Two Sections of 512th (London) Fd. Co. R.E. will relieve two Sections of 478th Field Co. R.E. at H.Q.C. on June 1st. They will be required for work on construction of dugouts for R.F.A. affiliated to Division in Right section.

2.   Two sections of 512th (London) Fd. Co. R.E. will relieve two sections of 478th Field Co. R.E. at N.12.a.2.2. on June 1st. They will be required for work on construction of dugouts for R.F.A. affiliated to Division in Left section.

3.   One Officer, ~~~~~~~~~~~~~~~~~~~~~ on the morning of 31st, to report to C.R.E. 57th Division to arrange with C.R.A. and C.R.E. 57th Division for taking over accommodation and work from two sections 478th Field Coy and to guide the sections in on June 1st.

4.   One Officer, ~~~~~~~~~~~~~~~~~~~~~ to report, on the morning of the 31st, to C.R.E. 59th Division to arrange with C.R.A. and C.R.E. 59th Division for taking over accommodation and work from two sections 478th Field Coy and to guide the sections in on June 1st.

Issued at 8-30 a.m.   Capt. & Adjt. R.E.
    31/5/17.   for C.R.E., 56th Division.

Copy No 1. 512th (London) Field Coy R.E.
        2. "G"
        3. 56th Divisional Train.
        4. War Diary.
        5. File.

Army Form C. 2118.

WAR DIARY
INTELLIGENCE SUMMARY.
(Erase heading not required.)

Headquarters
56th Div¹ R.E.

Place	Date 1917	Hour	Summary of Events and Information	Remarks and references to Appendices
HABARCQ	2/6		C.R.E. inspected 416 & 512 Field Coys and Hd.q'rs Section of Div¹ Signal Coy	
"	3/6		Casualties:- 513th Field Coy, wounded 2 O.Rs.	
"	4/6		G.O.C. Division inspected 416 & 512 Field Coys and Hd.q'rs Section of Div¹ Signal Coy.	
"	5/6		Received 56th Div¹ Order No. 101, stating that Rn Swanson will relieve the 61st Division in the line. Issued Order No. 103. Copy attached	A
"	6/6		C.R.E. visited C.R.E. 61st Division as to the taking over. Received 56th Div¹ Order No. 102	
"	7/6		Issued Amendment to Order No. 103. Copy attached.	B
"	8/6		C.R.E. visited BEAURAINS and ARRAS. Received Administrative Instructions in connection with 56th Div¹ Order No. 101.	
"	9/6		Received Amendment to 56th Div¹ Order No. 101	
"	10/6		C.R.E. visited front line	
"	11/6		Moved by road to billets in ARRAS.	

Army Form C. 2118.

WAR DIARY
or
INTELLIGENCE SUMMARY.
(Erase heading not required.)

Place	Date 1917	Hour	Summary of Events and Information	Remarks and references to Appendices
ARRAS	11/6		Received 56th Divl Order No 103	
"	12/6		C.R.E. worked from line	
"	13/6		C.R.E. visited 1/5th Cheshire Regiment	
			O.C. 513 Field Coy. came with reference to work on Coy Hdqtrs in the line	
"	14/6		C.R.E. worked from line	
			Received 56th Divl Order No 104	
"	16/6		C.R.E. visited G.O.C. 169th Infantry Brigade, also from line	
			Casualty 56th Divl Signal Coy. Wounded 1 O.R.	
"	17/6		Received 56th Divl Order No 105	
"	18/6		Forwarded "Proposed Scheme for repair of roads and pushing forward of R.E. dumps" as asked for in 56th Divl Order No 104. Copy attached.	C
			C.R.E. worked from line	
			Casualty 513 Field Coy. Wounded 1 O.R. at duty.	
"	19/6		C.R.E. visited from line with G.O.C. Division.	

WAR DIARY
or
INTELLIGENCE SUMMARY.
(Erase heading not required.)

Army Form C. 2118

Place	Date	Hour	Summary of Events and Information	Remarks and references to Appendices
ARRAS	20/6		Adjutant visited front line. CRE visited Corps H.Q. and front line, also held conference of O.s.C. Field Coys and discussed amongst other things scheme of training for when the Divn goes out of the line	
"	21/6		CRE visited front line	
"	23/6		CRE visited front line	
"			Received 56th Divl defence scheme	
"	25/6		CRE visited front line	
"	26/6		Received 56th Divl Order No. 106	
"	27/6		Received Amendment to 56th Divl Order No. 106	
"			Issued Order No. 104. Copy attached	
"			CRE! 12th and 50th Divisions came as to the taking over by them	
"	29/6		Adjutant left for England on 10 days leave and 2nd Lieut K.V. MORHAM arrived to act	
			Handed 512th Field Coy Hqrs. 89th Field Coy would relieve them	D

Army Form C. 2118

WAR DIARY
or
INTELLIGENCE SUMMARY.

(Erase heading not required.)

Instructions regarding War Diaries and Intelligence Summaries are contained in F. S. Regs., Part II. and the Staff Manual respectively. Title pages will be prepared in manuscript.

Place	Date 1917	Hour	Summary of Events and Information	Remarks and references to Appendices
ARRAS	29/6		Received 51st Div. Order No 107 and Administrative Instructions in connection with same. C.R.E. visited front line.	
"	30/6		Issued Order No 105, copy attached. Casualty 5th Field Coy. Wounded 1 O.R.	E

J. A. Tower
Lieut Col R.E.
C.R.E. 51st Division

SECRET.   Copy No. ......

56th Divisional Warning Order No. 103.

1.   56th Division are relieving 61st Division in the line on the night of 10/11th June.

2.   169th Infantry Brigade will be in the line.

3.   416th (Edinburgh) Field Coy R.E. will work with 169th Infantry Brigade.

4.   Moves of Field Companies and Pioneers will probably be as in attached table.

5.   ACKNOWLEDGE.

Issued at 5 p.m.
5/6/17.
                                             Capt. & Adjt. R.E.
                                        for C.R.E., 56th Division.

Copy No. 1. 416th (Edinburgh) Field Coy R.E.
         2. 512th (London) Field Coy R.E.
         3. 513th (London) Field Coy R.E.
         4. 1/5th Cheshire Regiment.
         5. "G"
         6. War Diary.
         7. File.

SECRET.

RELIEF TABLE to accompany Order No. 102.

Date	Unit	From	To	Relieving	Remarks
9th	219th Field Coy R.E.	GOUVES	Behind Citadel ARRAS		Moving from GOUVES at 6 a.m.; bivouac behind Citadel, ARRAS until 5-30 p.m.
9th	do. 2 sections.	Behind Citadel ARRAS	N.20.b.2.8.	89th Field Coy R.E.	Moving from Citadel at 5-30 p.m. Transport Lines at M.11.a.3.6. 1 Officer & 2 N.C.Os. to report to 89th Field Coy on 8th inst. to take over work.
9th	do. Headquarters & 2 sections.	do.	N.10.central	479th Field Coy R.E.	1 Officer & 2 N.C.Os. to report to 479th Field Coy on 8th inst. to take over work.
9th	1/5th Cheshire Regt. (less 2 Companies)	GOUVES	ARRAS		
10th	do.	ARRAS	N.16.b.3.5.	1/5th D.C.L.I. and 11th King's Liverpool Regiment.	1 Officer & 2 N.C.Os. to report to H.Q. 11th K.L. Regt. (N.12.b.5.5.) on 9th inst. to take over work. 1 Officer & 2 N.C.Os. to report to 1/5th D.C.L.I. (N.16.b.3.3.) on 9th inst.
10th	519th Field Coy R.E.	SIMENCOURT	N.8.d.8.8.	479th Field Coy R.E.	March with Brigade Group. Transport Lines at G.33.b.5.5. 1 Officer & 2 N.C.Os. to report to 479th Field Coy (N.8.d.8.8.) on 9th inst. to take over work.

SECRET.   Copy No. 5....

Amendment to 56th Divisional Engineers Order No. 103.

416th (Edinburgh) Field Coy R.E. will move under orders of the 169th Infantry Brigade, but Headquarters and the two sections relieving 479th Field Coy R.E. will not be able to get into billets at N.10.central until after 7-0 p.m. on the 10th instant.

Issued at 6-30 p.m.   Capt. & Adjt. R.E.
7/8/17.   for C.R.E., 56th Division.

Copy No. 1. 416th (Edinburgh) Field Coy R.E.
         2. C.R.E., 61st Division.
         3. "G"
         4. "Q"
         5. War Diary.
         6. File.

Headquarters,
    56th Division.

Reference Divisional Order No.104, para. 6 (c), the following is the proposed scheme for repair of roads and pushing forward of R.E. dumps :-

Road Material.
Dumps of road material should be established at once at WANCOURT (N.22.b.2.9.) and on the main CAMBRAI road (about O.7.c. 2.5.), each of these dumps should contain at least
- 2000 Pit Props or Sleepers.
- 1000 tons Road Metal.
- 3000 R & S Dogs.
- 12 Artillery Bridges.
- 50 Shovels.

Light Railways.
Sufficient material should be got forward to WANCOURT as soon as possible for extension of light railway as shewn on attached map.
It is presumed that the Light Railway Construction Company would carry out this extension.

Roads.
(1) In the event of an advance being made, a section of R.E. would proceed along WANCOURT-CHERISY Road as far as cross roads at O.25.central and thence towards VIS-EN-ARTOIS as far as possible. This section would clear and carry out all minor repairs to raods, making diversions round craters and other obstacles to allow Artillery to advance as quickly as possible. The Section Officer would make a thorough reconnaissance of the right sub-sector, reporting quantities of material required, and where required, to put roads in good condition for all transport.

(2) A Section of R.E. would advance along CAMBRAI Road and if road was not too badly damaged, would clear and carry out minor repairs, and make diversions where necessary, but no attempt would be made to fill craters.
If roadway was beyond rapid repairs, the section would site and peg out the best line for Fair Weather Track, South of, and parallel to, CAMBRAI Road as shewn on map.
A thorough reconnaissance would be made of the left sub-sector, and reports sent in giving quantities of material required to make roads fit for all transport.

Working Parties.
Two Companies of Pioneers would immediately be put to work on road described in (1).
Two Companies of Pioneers would be put to work on Fair Weather Track described in (2).
Pioneers would work on these two forward roads until they were in good condition for all horse transport.
When this was done, Pioneers would take on the repair to road leading from 0.21.c.7.7. along valley and parallel to CONJEUL RIVER, crossing river near GUEMAPPE, and thence to WANCOURT. This would make a complete circuit for both sub-sectors.
Remainders of R.E.s would be employed on repairs to Bridges and any other work of immediate importance during advance.

R.E. Dumps.

The MARLIER Dump (map reference N.23.b.35.80.) will become the main Divisional Dump and should be fed direct from Corps Park, either by rail as at present or by motor lorries.

Attached list shows reserve of stores that would be kept at this point.

Forward Dumps.

Two forward dumps would be established at O.20.d.4.4. and O.15.c.4.5. These dumps would be fed from MARLIERE Dump, either by rail or by horse transport.

Attached list shows stores that would be kept at these dumps.

Lieut.Col.R.E.,
C.R.E., 56th Division.

18/6/17.

Divisional R.E. Dump.

STORES.	QUANTITY.
Sandbags.	75,000.
Shovels G.S.	3,000.
Picks & Helves.	1,000.
Spun Yarn.	5 cwt.
Tracing Tapes.	100. rolls.
Trench Boards.	200.
Screw Post Long.	2,000.
" " Medium.	750.
Pickets wood 6' & 3'.	300. each.
Barbed wire.	500. coils.
French Wire.	30 bundles.
Staples F.W.E.	5. boxes.
Hedging Gloves.	100. pairs.
Pliers wirecutting.	100. pairs.
Rifle wirecutters.	50. pairs.
Loophole plates.	20.
Dugouts Elephant (or equiv. in cupolas.	2. complete.
Rails 12' to 14'.	20.
Joists 9'.	20.
Pitprops 6" to 9".	40.
Corrugated iron.	1,000. sheets.
Crow bars.	10.
Mauls & Helves.	15.
Dogs 12".	300.
Nails 6",5",4",3",2", & 1".	4. cwts. each.
" Clout.	2. "
Screws 3", 2", & 1".	2. gross each.
Paint black, white & red.	1. cwt. each.
Paint brushes.	6.
Cordage 2".	2. coils.
Wire netting.	50. rolls.
Felt.	50. rolls.
Canvas.	5. rolls.
Wire plain.	20. coils.
Axes hand.	20.
Saws hand.	10.
Bill hooks.	10.
9" x 3" & 5" x 3".	2,000. f.r. each.
4" x 2".	4,000. f.r. each.
Forest 1½".	2,000. f.r. each.
Boarding 1".	2,000. f.r. each.

For Artillery.

Rails 15'	30.
Coir Netting.	4. rolls.
Pitprops 9".	20.

Guncotton.	100. slabs.
Primers.	5. boxes.
Detonators. No.8.	2. small boxes.
Safety Fuse.	2. tins.

The Two Advanced R.E. Dumps.

STORES.	QUANTITY.
Screw Pickets Long.	1,500.
" " Short.	600.
Barbed Wire.	400. coils.
French :	30. "
Sandbags.	25,000.
Shovels.	1,000.
Picks & Helves.	800.
Plain wire.	35. coils.
Wirecutters pliers.	20. pairs.
Tracing Tape.	50. rolls.
Mauls & Helves.	n 30.
Loophole plates.	45.
Pickets wood 3½'.	400.
Trench Bridges Infy.	20.
Wire netting.	20. rolls.
Nails 6",4",3" &2".	2. cwts. each.
Saws hand.	10.
Hammers hand.	10.
Axes felling.	10.
Axes hand.	10.
Canvas.	2. rolls.
Spun yarn.	2. bundles.
Cordage 2".	1. coil.

SECRET. Copy No...4...

56th Divisional Engineers Order No. 104.

1. The 513th (London) Field Coy R.E. (less two sections) will move to GRAND RULLECOURT on the 28th instant.

2. Rations for 48 hours will be carried.

Ration indent for 30th instant will be handed to Town Major, AVESNES LE COMTE AS THE Company passes through there, and arrangements made with him for drawing the rations.

3. No restrictions as to route, but Company will arrive at GRAND RULLECOURT by 3 p.m. in order to offload two lorry loads of stores which are being delivered there.

4. Billets will be allotted by the Billet Warden, GRAND RULLECOURT.

Issued at 4-15 p.m.
27th June, 1917.

Capt. & Adjt. R.E.
for C.R.E., 56th Division.

Copy No. 1. 513th (London) Field Coy R.E.
 2. "G"
 3. "Q"
 4. War Diary.
 5. File.

SECRET.   Copy No...5...

56th Divisional Engineers Order No. 105.

1.   At 12 noon on 2nd July, 56th Division will be transferred to VII Corps; the Inter-Corps boundary between VII and XVII Corps will then be that described in para. 1 of 56th Divn. Order No.106 of 26th inst., produced as far West as the ARRAS-BOIRY STe RICTRUDE Road, with the exception that GORDON ALLEY has now been made inclusive to XVII Corps.

2.   56th Division (less Artillery) will be relieved between 2nd and 4th July, 1917, by 50th Division.

3.   50th Division is arranging for 1 Coy R.E. and 2 Coys Pioneers to move to about H.15 and H.14 respectively on 1st July in order to take over work in the line from 2nd July (inclusive).

        C.R.E. will arrange to hand over to C.R.E., 50th Division all necessary details of work in the area for which he is responsible.

4.   Div. H.Q. will close at ARRAS on 4th July, and open at the CHATEAU, LE CAUROY, at the same hour.

5.   The following distances will be maintained on the march West of ARRAS :-

        250 yards between Battalions.
        100 yards between Companies or Sections of Transport.

6.   ACKNOWLEDGE
        The 87th Field Coy R.E., 12th Division, will take over work North of GORDON ALLEY on night of 1st/2nd July. The Os. C. the two Coys will arrange relief, which must be completed by morning of 2nd July.

Issued at 10 a.m.   Lieut. Col. R.E.
30th July, 1917.   C.R.E., 56th Division.

Copy No. 1. 512th (London) Field Coy R.E.
         2. 513th (London) Field Coy R.E.
         3. 416th (Edinburgh) Field Coy R.E.
         4. "G"
         5. War Diary.
         6. File.

MARCH TABLE TO ACCOMPANY 56th DIVISIONAL ENGINEERS ORDER No. 105.

Serial No.	Date July	Unit	From	To	Route	Remarks.
8	3rd	1/5th Cheshire Regt. 193rd Div. M.G. Coy. 512th Field Coy R.E. 513th Field Coy R.E. (less 2 sections) 416th Field Coy R.E.	Present Billets	GOUY	WAILLY-BEAUMETZ	No restrictions. Under the command of O.C. 1/5th Cheshire Regt.
9	4th	1/5th Cheshire Regt. 193rd Div. M.G. Coy. 512th Field Coy R.E. 513th Field Coy R.E. (less 2 sections) 416th Field Coy R.E.	GOUY	GRAND MELICOURT SARS-LEZ-BOIS SOMBRIN	FOSSEUX-BARLY	No restriction. Under the command of O.C. 1/5th Cheshire Regt.

Army Form C. 2118

WAR DIARY
or
INTELLIGENCE SUMMARY.
(Erase heading not required.)

Headquarters
56th Divisional R.E.

WO 18

Instructions regarding War Diaries and Intelligence Summaries are contained in F.S. Regs., Part II. and the Staff Manual respectively. Title pages will be prepared in manuscript.

Place	Date 1917	Hour	Summary of Events and Information	Remarks and references to Appendices
ARRAS	2/7		C.R.E. visited C.R.E. 12th Division. C.R.E. 50th Division came, and the handing over of all papers in connection with the relief was completed.	
"	4/7		At noon today the Division came under the orders of VIIth Corps.	
SOMBRIN	5/7		Moved by road to SOMBRIN for training. Sergt Major instructors lent by Division to instruct in Bayonet Fighting & Physical Training. C.R.E. went on leave to England.	
"	10/7		Major G.T. KINGSFORD, 513th Field Coy R.E. arrived to act. Adjutant returned from leave and 2nd Lieut K.N. MORHAM returned to unit.	
"	14/7		Received Administrative Instructions No 1 in connection with the move from the LE CAUROY area	
"	19/7		Received Administrative Instructions No 2 and 3. Received 56th Divisional Order No 108. Issued Order No 106. Copy attached	A

WAR DIARY
or
INTELLIGENCE SUMMARY.

(Erase heading not required.)

Army Form C. 2118

Place	Date	Hour	Summary of Events and Information	Remarks and references to Appendices
	1917			
SOMBRIN	20/7		C.R.E. returned from leave.	
			Major G.T. KINGSFORD returned to unit.	
	21/7		Received Administrative Instruction No 4	
			Received Administrative Instruction No 5	
			Received 56th Divisional Order No 109.	
			Issued Order No 107. Copy attached	B
	24/7		Moved by road to FRÉVENT, entrained to ARQUES, detrained and marched to billets at EPERLECQUES, coming under the orders of VIII Corps, Fifth Army.	
EPERLECQUES	25/7 to 31/7		Companies occupied in training, more especially in Pontooning. Also on improvements to the area under the Chief Engineer.	

Lt. Col. R.E.
C.R.E. 56th DIV. ENG.

SECRET. Copy No. 5....

56th. DIVISIONAL ENGINEERS' ORDER No. 106.

Ref. Map 1/100,000 LENS.

1. 56th. Division (less Artillery), accompanied by Divisional Supply Column and A.C. Cable Section, is being transferred from VII Corps, Third Army, to Fifth Army.

2. 56th. Division (less Artillery) and A.C. Cable Section will move by rail; the entrainment will commence at any time after midnight 22nd/23rd July. Orders for entrainment will be issued separately.

3. The Divisional Supply Column will move by road under orders to be issued later.

4. A.C. Cable Section will be attached to H.Q. 56th. Division Signal Coy. and will arrive at LE CAUROY by 4 p.m. 22nd. instant.

5. To facilitate entrainment, moves will be carried out on 22nd inst. in accordance with the attached March Table.

6. Rations will be carried for the day following the day of entrainment.

   Supply Railheads will be notified later.

7. ACKNOWLEDGE.

Issued at 8 p.m.
on 19/7/17.

Capt. & Adjt., R.E.,
for C.R.E., 56th. Division.

Copy No. 1. 512th. Field Coy.
        2. 513th. Field Coy.
        3. 416th. Field Coy.
        4. "Q".
        5. War Diary.
        6. File.

MARCH TABLE issued with Bath. Divisional Engineers' Order No. 106.

Serial No.	Date.	Unit.	From	To	Route & Remarks.
4.	22nd July.	518th I B Field Coy. R.E.	SOMBRIN.	MONCHEAUX.	Via LIENCOURT – ETREE-WAMIN – HOUVIN – HOUVIGNEUL. To be clear of LIENCOURT by 10-30 a.m. To march under orders of R.S.G. 188th Infantry Brigade.
6.	22nd July.	416th Field Coy. R.E.	SOMBRIN.	TINCVILLE & BERICOURT.	Via IVERGNY – BERNEVILLE – BENBRUVE – MONVAL. To be clear of IVERGNY by 10 a.m. To march under orders of R.S.C. 187th Infantry Brigade.
7.	22nd July	515th Field Coy. R.E.	SOMBRIN.	BOUCHMAISON.	Via SUS – IVERGNY. To march under orders of R.S.C. 189th Infantry Brigade. Not to enter IVERGNY before 10-15 a.m.

SECRET.   Copy No...4...

56th. Divisional Engineers' Order No. 107.

Ref. Map 1/100,000, HAZEBROUCK.

1.   In continuation of 56th. Divisional Engineers' Order
No. 106 of 19th inst., units, on arrival at detraining
stations, will move to billets in accordance with the
attached table.

2.   ACKNOWLEDGE.

Issued at 6 p.m. on   Lieut-Colonel, R.E.,
21/7/17.   C.R.E., 56th. Division.

Copy No. 1. 512th. Field Co. R.E.
         2. 513th. Field Co. R.E.
         3. 416th. Field Co. R.E.
         4. War Diary. ✓
         5. File.

MARCH TABLE ISSUED WITH 56th DIVISIONAL ENGINEERS' ORDER No. 107.

Serial No.	Date.	Unit.	From detraining Statn.	To	Route.	Remarks.
1.	JULY 23rd & 24th.	Div. Employment Coy. Div. H.Q., & Depot Bn. Div. Sig. Co. A.C. Cable Section. Div. Engineers H.Q.	ARQUES	EPERLECQUES	No restrictions.	Each train load moves off independantly under the orders of O.C. Train Load as soon after detrainment as possible.
2.	23rd & 24th.	169th Bde. Group.	ST. OMER.	MOULLE Area.	ST.MARTIN-TILQUES MOULLE.	-do-
3.	-do-	193rd M.G.Coy. H.Q. Div. Train. Mob.Vet.Section.	-do-	EPERLECQUES.	-do-	-do-
4.	-do-	167th Bde. Group.	ARQUES.	MOULLE Area.	Southern outskirts of ST.OMER - ST. MARTIN - TILQUES - MOULLE.	-do-
5.	-do-	168th Bde. Group. (Including 1/5th Cheshire Regt.)	WIZERNES.	EPERLECQUES Area.	Not to enter ST. OMER - otherwise no restrictions.	Billets for night 23rd/24th at WIZERNES. Move to EPERLECQUES Area on 24th under the orders of G.O.C. 168th Inf. Bde. No Unit to cross the ST.OMER - NORDAUSQUES Road before 10 a.m. 24th inst.

Army Form C. 211

WAR DIARY
or
INTELLIGENCE SUMMARY.
(Erase heading not required.)

Headquarters
56th Divl. R.E.

Vol 19

Place	Date	Hour	Summary of Events and Information	Remarks and references to Appendices
	1914			
EPERLECQUES	3/8		C.R.E. attended conference at Divl. H.Q. Received warning order that the Divn. will be prepared to move on 5th & 6th.	
"	4/8		Also to be prepared to send H16th Field Co. by route march on 4th to next area. Received orders that transport of H16th Field Co. will move today to NOORDPEENE, proceeding tomorrow to STEENVOORDE. Warning order received that H.Q. Transport will move on 5th to NOORDPEENE. Received 56th Divl. Order No. 110.	
"	5/8		Transport moved by road to NOORDPEENE.	
"	6/8		Transport proceeded to RENINGHELST. Dismounted personnel entrained at WATTEN, proceeded to ABEELE, and marched to RENINGHELST, coming under orders of II nd Corps.	
RENINGHELST	7/8		Warned that this Divn. will probably relieve the 12th Divn.	
	8/8		C.R.E. visited Sec.R.E. 12th Divn. Capt. A.B. Murray R.A.M.C. (T) posted for duty with Divl. R.E. vice Capt. L. Straw resigned.	
"	9/8		Received 56th Divl. Instructions No. 1.	

Army Form C. 2118.

WAR DIARY
or
INTELLIGENCE SUMMARY.
(Erase heading not required.)

Instructions regarding War Diaries and Intelligence Summaries are contained in F.S. Regs., Part II. and the Staff Manual respectively. Title pages will be prepared in manuscript.

Place	Date	Hour	Summary of Events and Information	Remarks and references to Appendices
	1917			
RENINGHELST.	11/8		Received 56th Divl. Orders 111 & 112.	
"	12/8		Issued Orders No. 108 & 109 (copies attached).	
			Issued 56th Divl. Engnrs. Order No.110 (copy attached)	
			Received 56th Divl. Administrative Instruction No.1. in connection with the relief of 18th Divn.	
			Received instructions that 1 Coy. of 1/5th Cheshire Regt. will relieve Pioneer Coy. of 11th South Lancs Regt., 30th Divn. working under A.D.L.R. 2. on railway construction on 13th inst.	
			Issued orders to 513th and 416th Field Coys to take over from outgoing Field Coys and to get in touch with the Brigades.	
			Ordered 416th Field Coy. to clean the YPRES - MENIN Road between the Culvert + HOOGE and to make a turning point at HOOGE.	
			Received 56th Divl. Instructions No. 2.	
"	13/8		Moved by road to DICKEBUSCH.	
			Ordered 1/5th Cheshire Regt. to detail 1 platoon for work at Dump.	
			Issued Order No. 111 (copy attached)	

WAR DIARY
INTELLIGENCE SUMMARY.
(Erase heading not required.)

Army Form C. 2118

Place	Date	Hour	Summary of Events and Information	Remarks and references to Appendices
	1917			
RENINGHELST	13/8 cont.		Received 56th Divnl. Order No. 113 and Instructions No. 3. C.R.A. held a conference with the O's i/c the 2 Field Coys. detailed for the coming operations.	
DICKEBUSCH	14/8		Received 56th Divnl. Order No. 113. Casualties:- 513th Field Coy. Killed 1 O.R. Wounded 1 O.R. " 416th " " " " 3 O.R. " " " " " 1 O.R. C.R.E. visited forward area with Bde. Major of Artillery to inspect artillery tracks, afterwards going to C.C. II nd Corps on the same subject. Issued Order No. 112 (copy attached) Received 56th Divnl. Instructions No. 4.	
"	15/8		Received 56th Divnl. Orders No. 114, 115 and Instructions No. 5. Issued Order No. 113 (copy attached)	
"	16/8		Instructed 512th Field Coy that they will be at disposal of 168th Brigade until further orders. Casualty: 2 Lieut. K.N. Wenham, 416th Field Co.M.C. wounded.	

Army Form C. 2118

WAR DIARY
or
INTELLIGENCE SUMMARY.
(Erase heading not required.)

Instructions regarding War Diaries and Intelligence Summaries are contained in F. S. Regs., Part II. and the Staff Manual respectively. Title pages will be prepared in manuscript.

Place	Date	Hour	Summary of Events and Information	Remarks and references to Appendices
	1917			
DICKEBUSCH	17/8		Issued Orders No. 114, 115 & 116 (Leapins attacked) Casualties:- 116th Field Co. R.E. Killed 4 O.R., Wounded 11 O.R. Missing 2 O.R. Received 56th Divl. Orders 116 & 117.	
"	18/8		Moved by road to RENINGHELST.	
RENINGHELST	19/8		Asked for Training Programmes from the Field Companies.	
"	20/8		Received orders from 56 Divn. that 512th (London) Field Co. R.E. will be placed at disposal of G.O.C. 2nd Corps, for work at Workshops, BUSSEBOOM. R.E. held a conference with O's. C. Field Cos. Casualty - 56th Divl. Signal Co. Wounded (aircraft) 1 O.R. Received warning from 56 Divn. that the Divn. will probably move by rail (Transport by Road) at short notice.	
"	21/8		1 Company of 1/5th Cheshire Regt. placed at disposal of G.O.C., 14th Divn. and 1 Company at disposal of G.O.C. 44th Divn.	
"	22/8		Issued Order No. 114 (body attacked)	
"	23/8		Transport moved by road from RENINGHELST and rested for the night at ARNEKE.	

Army Form C. 2118

WAR DIARY
or
INTELLIGENCE SUMMARY.
(Erase heading not required.)

Instructions regarding War Diaries and Intelligence Summaries are contained in F.S. Regs., Part II. and the Staff Manual respectively. Title pages will be prepared in manuscript.

Place	Date	Hour	Summary of Events and Information	Remarks and references to Appendices
	1917			
REMINGHELST	24/8		Transport arrived at EPERLECQUES.	
			Personnel moved by rail to WATTEN and marched to EPERLECQUES.	
			Div came under orders of VIth Corps.	
EPERLECQUES	25/8		Transport of 512th Field Co. moved by road en route for BLUE MAISON.	
	26/8		Transport of 512th Field Co. arrived BLUE MAISON.	
			Personnel of 512th Field Co. moved to BLUE MAISON by train.	
	27/8		Received warning from 56th Div. that Div. will probably move to Third Army starting 30th inst.	
	28/8		Received 56th Div. O.120	
			Issued O.118 (copy attached)	
			Received Entraining Instructions.	
	30/8		Moved by road to ST. OMER, and entrained at 10.40 p.m.	
FREMICOURT	31/8		Arrived BAPAUME, detrained, and marched to FREMICOURT.	
			Division came under orders of IVth Corps (Third Army)	

[signature]
Lt. Col. R.E.
C.R.E. 60th DIV. ENGRS

Army Form C. 211

WAR DIARY
of
INTELLIGENCE SUMMARY.
(Erase heading not required.)

Headquarters, 56th Div. R.E.

Vol 20

Place	Date	Hour	Summary of Events and Information	Remarks and references to Appendices
FRENICOURT	1917			
	1/9		Received 56th Div Order No 122. Issued Order No 119. (Copy attached)	A
			C.R.E. visited C.R.E. 3rd Div. and arranged the relief of Area Boyelles.	
"	2/9		Received Amendment to 56th Div Order No 122. 513th Field Coy (less transport) moved to ROCQUIGNY to commence work on Corps Rifle Range.	
			C.R.E. visited C.R.E. 3rd Div.	
"	3/9		Issued Amendment to Order No 119. Copy attached. Marred 1/5th checkered that they will relieve KRRC (Pioneers) on the night 4/5th.	B
			C.R.E. attended Conference at Div Hdqrs.	
"	4/9		C.R.E. visited the line with C.R.E. 3rd Div. 2nd Lieut R. ORR, 416th Field Coy R.E. took up the duties of Officer i/c Ruthy and Horse Standings.	
"	5/9		C.R.E. visited 513th Field Coy	
"	6/9		C.R.E. visited the three Field Coys	

WAR DIARY

INTELLIGENCE SUMMARY.

(Erase heading not required.)

Army Form C. 2118

Instructions regarding War Diaries and Intelligence Summaries are contained in F. S. Regs., Part II. and the Staff Manual respectively. Title pages will be prepared in manuscript.

Place	Date	Hour	Summary of Events and Information	Remarks and references to Appendices
	1919			
FREMICOURT	2/9		C.R.E. visited C.R.E. 3rd Divn and took over all papers and plans in connection with the relief.	
"	5/9		C.R.E. visited forward area	
			Chief Engineer, IVth Corps Came with reference to the work in hand	
"	9/9		C.R.E. visited forward area	
"	10/9		– do –	
"	12/9		C.R.E. visited forward area to inspect site of the proposed push tramway	
"	15/9		C.R.E. with Tramway Officer, visited new site for the tramway	
"	19/9		C.R.E. held a Conference of O.s.C. Field Coys	
"			C.R.E. visited Chief Engineer IV Corps	
"	20/9		C.R.E. visited site of the new tramway	
"	21/9		C.R.E. visited forward area	
"	28/9		C.R.E. visited forward area with DM90 & Camouflage Officer	

WAR DIARY

INTELLIGENCE SUMMARY.

Army Form C. 2118

Place	Date	Hour	Summary of Events and Information	Remarks and references to Appendices
FREMICOURT	1919 30/9		C.R.E. inspected the under huttings and horse standings of the division. The Field Companies have been fully employed during the month on dugouts in the Welwedrale Line and in preparing winter quarters for men and horses in the back area.	

J.A. Frere Lt Col
Lt Col
C.R.E. 5th Div

SECRET.   Copy No. 8

56th DIVISIONAL ENGINEERS' ORDER No. 119.

Reference Sheet 57C 1/40,000.

1. The 56th Division (less Artillery) will relieve the 3rd Division (less Artillery) in the line.

2. (a) The 168th, 169th, and 167th Infantry Brigades will relieve the 9th, 8th, and 76th Infantry Brigades respectively on the nights 5/6th, 6/7th, and 7/8th September.

3. The 512th, 513th, and 416th Field Companies R.E. will relieve the 56th, 438th, and 529th Field Companies R.E. on September 5th, September 6th, and September 7th respectively.
   H.Q. of all three Field Companies are in LEBUCQUIERE.
   56th Division Field Companies will not arrive at their new billets till after 12 noon on the above dates.

4. 2 Officers and 2 N.C.O's. from each of the 512th, 513th, and 416th Field Companies R.E. will report at the billets of 56th, 438th, and 529th Field Companies R.E. on September 2nd to take over particulars of work, etc. These Officers and N.C.O's will be billeted and rationed by 3rd Division Field Companies.

5. One Officer per Company of 1/5th Cheshire Regt. will report at Company Billets of 20th K.R.R.C. (Pioneers) on September 2nd to take over particulars of work etc.
   These Officers will be rationed and billeted by 20th K.R.R.C.
   H.Q. of 20th K.R.R.C.   J.20.d.2.4.
   "A" Company   I.11.d central.
   "B", "C", & "D" Companies   BEAUMETZ.

6. Date of relief of 20th K.R.R.C. by 1/5th Cheshire Regt. will be notified later.

7. Strict attention will be paid to March Discipline and Field Companies will march by sections.

8. Defence Schemes, maps, Aeroplane photos, Dumps, Trench Stores, etc. will be taken over on relief.

9. Completion of relief to be reported to this Office.

10. Divisional R.E. H.Q. will remain at FREMICOURT.

11. ACKNOWLEDGE.

Issued at 6 p.m.   Lieut-Colonel, R.E.,
on 1/9/17.   C.R.E., 56th Division.

Copy No. 1 512th Field Co. R.E.
         2 513th Field Co. R.E.
         3 416th Field Co. R.E.
         4 1/5th Cheshire Regt.
         5 "G".
         6 C.R.E., 3rd Divn.
         7 56th Div. Train.
         8 War Diary.
         9 File.

SECRET.   Copy No....8....

Amendment to
56th DIVISIONAL ENGINEERS' ORDER No. 119.
----

1. Reliefs mentioned in para. 3 of 56th Divisional Engineers' Order No. 119 will take place 24 hours earlier.

2. Command of Divisional front will pass to G.O.C., 56th Division, at 10 a.m. 7th September, by which hour the relief of all units of 3rd Division (less Artillery) will be complete.

3. ACKNOWLEDGE.

Issued at 11 a.m.   Lieut-Colonel, R.E.,
on 3/9/17.   C.R.E., 56th Division.

Copy No. 1 512th (London) Field Co. R.E.
         2 513th (London) Field Co. R.E.
         3 416th (Edinr.) Field Co. R.E.
         4 1/5th Cheshire Regt.
         5 "G"
         6 C.R.E., 3rd Division.
         7 56th Div. Train.
         8 War Diary.
         9 File.

WAR DIARY

INTELLIGENCE SUMMARY.

Army Form C. 2118.

Hdqrs, 56th Div R.E.

Vol 21

Place	Date	Hour	Summary of Events and Information	Remarks and references to Appendices
	1917 Oct.			
FREMICOURT	14/10		Orders received that Lieut Col H.N. GORDON, D.S.O. had been appointed Chief Engineer IV Corps, and that Lieut Col E.N. MOZLEY, D.S.O. had been appointed C.R.E. 56th Div.	
"	15/10		Lieut Col E.N. MOZLEY arrived to take over	
"	16/10		Lieut Col H.N. GORDON left for 1st Corps.	
			During the month the Field Companies have been fully occupied chiefly on the defence of the Intermediate Line of the division, largely consisting of making mined dug-outs. A large amount of track area accommodation was also constructed.	

Mozley
Lt Col: R.E.
C.R.E. 56TH DIVL ENGRS

Army Form C. 2118.

WAR DIARY
—or—
INTELLIGENCE SUMMARY.
(Erase heading not required.)

51st Aus R E Hdq/1/c.

WK22

Place	Date	Hour	Summary of Events and Information	Remarks and references to Appendices
FRENICOURT	1917 Nov.			
	1 to 16		Companies were only doing very urgent work in the forward area. Every available man was training in bridging	
	17 to 20		Work principally on the BAPAUME - CAMBRAI Road repairing and making diversions round craters	
	21		416th Field Coy erected temporary bridge over CANAL DU NORD on the BAPAUME - CAMBRAI Road. 513th Field Coy erected temporary bridge over CANAL DU NORD on the BAPAUME - CAMBRAI Road South of the one erected yesterday. Both these bridges were for Field Guns and Infantry in towing.	
	23		I attach copy of Report I have rendered to Div Hq/rs giving the work done by the Field Companies during the month.	

Murphy
Lt. Col. R.E.
C.R.E. 50th DIVL ENGS

H.Q. "G" 56th Divn.

In reply to G.3/602 of 4th December, the following narative is forwarded :-

1. Prior to 20th November, the Field Companies under my Command were employed as follows :-

   (a) From about 6th November, about 2 Sections per Company (in rotation) were struck off work for training, principally in Trestle Bridging but also in Engineer duties in mobile warfare such as :- Reconnaissance, Map reading, Compass work, hasty demolitions, etc.

   (b) From night of 16/17th inclusive for 4 nights, 2 Companies were employed with practically all the Pioneer Battalion and about 200 Infantry in corduroying the Northern side of the road from BEUGNY to BOURSIES.

   (c) In the meantime, it was necessary to collect and send forward by road and rail, and unloaded at selected dumps at LOUVERVAL, BEUGNY and LAGNICOURT a large amount of R.E. material, principally for road work and also for bridging, water supply, demolitions and Field fortifications in case of an advance. An average of 20 G.S. wagons daily and also 15 Light Railway trucks daily were thus sent forward.

2. The following is the diary of employment of the Divisional Engineers from 20th onwards (1 Section was detailed from the contro of C.R.E. to each Brigade and did not rejoin until 26 November):-

   20th November, 1917.

   416th Field Co. R.E: 1 Section employed on laying corduroy track on BEUGNY-BOURSIES Road. 2 Sections standing by with Trestle Bridge awaiting orders to go forward and erect it on site where BAPAUME-CAMBRAI Road crosses CANAL DU NORD. This site was in German hands up to 8 a.m. 20th November when the main bridge there was blown up as the enemy retreated. The same afternoon, 2 Officers and 3 O.Rs. of this Company reconnoitred the site of their proposed bridge.

   512th Field Co. R.E: 3 Sections corduroying BEUGNY-BOURSIES Road. An Officer of this Company went forward on this day to reconnoitre the CAMBRAI Road up to the Canal to ascertain the amount of work required to make it good for all Horse Transport.

   513th Field Co. R.E: 3 Sections employed on corduroy work and widening the BEUGNY-BOURSIES Road. One Officer and 2 O.R. with 1 nOfficer of the Q.W.R. reconnoitred in the afternoon the Road from DEMICOURT to the Canal du Nord at K.9.b.3.9. and were the first to reach and report upon the important Tramway Bridge, left intact by the Germans at K.9.b.3.9. This party incidentally took 14 prisoners during the reconnaissance.

   21st November, 1917.

   416th Field Co. R.E: 2 Sections continued corduroying main road. 1 Section continued standing by their Bridge material, which was loaded up ready to move off at a moment's notice.

   512th Field Co. R.E: On the night following this day, 3 Sections of the Company were employed with a Company of the Pioneers corduroying around the crater on the LAGNICOURT, QUEANT Road between our Intermediate and Front Lines. No. 1 Section (with Brigade) was employed in screening the roads and tracks on the LOUVERVAL-INCHY Road "No-mans Land".

   513th Field Co. R.E.

- 2 -

513th Field Co. R.E: 3 Sections employed on corduroying BEUGNY-BOURSIES Road. 1 Section standing by their load-ed up bridge.

22nd November, 1917.

416th Field Co. R.E: During the night of the 22nd, 2 Sections of this Company erected a plank Trestle Bridge across the CANAL DU NORD at E.27.c.1.4, which is North of the demolished Main Bridge.
The 3rd Section was employed on road work between BOURSIES and CANAL DU NORD under Major Gedge R.E. who was in charge of the repair of this stretch of road with the following troops under his command :-
1 Section of 416th Field Co. R.E.
1 Section of 512th Field Co. R.E.
2 Companies of Pioneers.

512th Field Co. R.E: 3 Sections employed on LAGNICOURT-QUEANT Road.

513th Field Co. R.E: 2 Sections stood by their Transport loaded with Bridging material. 1 Section employed on repair of the road from BOURSIES to CANAL DU NORD.

23rd November, 1917.

416th Field Co. R.E: A repair party of 2 N.C.Os. and 6 Sappers was left on the Bridge made the previous night. The Section which had been attached to the 167th Infantry Brigade rejoined the Company, and during the night of the 23rd, together with another section were employed on laying corduroy approaches to the Bridge. The 2 Sections which had been working the previous night (out for 16 hours) rested.

512th Field Co. R.E: The 3 Sections which had been on the LAGNICOURT-QUEANT Road were now transferred to quarters in BOURSIES and worked on this, and following nights on the road from BOURSIES to CANAL DU NORD. The 4th Section (with 168th Infantry Brigade) was employed by that Brigade on clearing roads across "No-mans Land" and siting new Communication Trenches from our new advanced positions.

513th Field Co. R.E: On the evening of this day, 2 Sections made a timber Trestle Bridge across the CANAL DU NORD at E.27.c.1.4. South of the demolished main Bridge. The 3rd Section worked on the road from BOURSIES to the CANAL.

24th November, 1917.

416th Field Co. R.E: 3 Sections employed on road from BOURSIES to CANAL, widening the road by laying corduroy on the Northern edge. The 4th Section completed corduroy approaches to the Bridge built across the CANAL.

512th Field Co. R.E: 2 Sections working on craters working on craters between BOURSIES and CANAL. 1 Section making splinter-proof quarters for the Company in BOURSIES, which was being heavily shelled. The Section with the Brigade was employed making Bombing Blocks for the London Scottish in the Hindenburg Line.

513th Field Co. R.E: 3 Sections employed corduroying road East of BOURSIES. Section with Brigade employed wiring and improving the Communication Trenches. A repair party of 1 N.C.O. and 6 men were left in charge of the Bridge. 1 Pioneer Coy. worked with each Field Coy.

25th November, 1917.

416th Field Co. R.E: The whole Company was employed on this night on widening and improving the road East of BOURSIES.

512th Field Co. R.E: The Section with the Brigade continued Bombing Blocks and other trench improvements in the new front line. 2 Sections worked on widening the BOURSIES-CAMBRAI Road by corduroying on the Northern side. 1 Section rest and baths.

513th Field Co. R.E: 3 Sections employed on widening road East of BOURSIES with corduroy.

1 Pioneer Coy. worked with each Field Coy.

26th November, 1917.

The Division having been transferred to new Corps, the work on the main CAMBRAI Road East of BOURSIES was handed over by C.R.E., 56th Division to C.R.E., 2nd Division. The Divisional R.E. were henceforward employed with the Pioneers for Brigades, except half of the 416th Field Co. R.E. which was working under C.R.E. on road screens. The repair parties of the 2 new bridges across the CANAL were now withdrawn. These repair parties had had an immense amount of work to do on these bridges, especially that of the 416th Field Co. R.E. which had on occasions been heavily shelled.

416th Field Co. R.E: 3 Sections preparing and erecting road screens on BAPAUME-CAMBRAI Road and BEAUMETZ-DOIGNIES Road. 1 Section commenced construction of mined dug-outs at D.24.c.7.9. for Battalion H.Q. of 168th Infantry Brigade.

512th Field Co. R.E: All 4 Sections employed this night on digging a Communication Trench near PICCADILLY (across old "No-man's Land").

513th Field Co. R.E: All 4 Sections employed on wiring part of new front line and new support line in Hindenburg Line and supervising digging of new Communication Trenches.

27th November, 1917.

416th Field Co. R.E: 2 Sections screening as before. 2 Sections working on dug-out at D.24.c.7.9. all round the clock, no Infantry carrying parties being available.

512th Field Co. R.E: All 4 Sections employed in wiring the Left Defensive Flank from TADPOLE COPSE, together and back in a South-Westerly direction to old front line wire.

513th Field Co. R.E: Work as on previous night.

28th November, 1917.

416th Field Co. R.E: Work as on previous night.

512th Field Co. R.E: Work as on previous night.

513th Field Co. R.E: Work as on previous night.

29th November, 1917.

416th Field Co. R.E: Work as on previous night.

512th Field Co. R.E: Work as on previous night.

513th Field Co. R.E: All 4 Sections employed on construction of dug-outs in reserve line in old enemy's outpost line for Right and Left Battalion H.Q. and in deepening reserve line for inter-communication.

30th November, 1917.

416th Field Co. R.E: 2 Sections moved from quarters in LEBUCQUIERE to billet at I.26.b.0.3. continuing work on screens. 2 Sections continued work on dug-out at D.24.c.7.9. and at J.3.a.2.6.

512th Field Co. R.E: 3 Sections employed in digging Strong Points in rear of TADPOLE RESERVE Wire. 4th Section resting.

513th Field Co. R.E: Work as on previous night.

1st December, 1917.

416th Field Co. R.E

- 4 -

<u>416th Field Co. R.E</u>: 2 Sections sent to work on dug-outs at D.24.c.7.9. but as a strong hostile attack was made on this day, the R.E. working party were employed as ammunition carriers for Infantry. 2 Sections sent to work under O.C. 4th London Regt. on siting and digging o... in D.23.

<u>512th Field Co. R.E</u>: Work as on previous night.

<u>513th Field Co. R.E</u>: After repulse of enemy counter-attack, the Company was employed during the night in wiring the reserve line for use as a new support line for 169th Infantry Brigade.

3 Companies Pioneers sent as fighting troops to 169 Bde. 1 Coy. similarly to 168th Bde.

<u>2nd December, 1917.</u>

<u>416th Field Co. R.E</u>: On night 1/2nd, 1 Section enlarge shallow trenches at D.29.b.7.7. and constructed 2 splinter-proof shelters there for reserve Battalion H.Q.. Another Section erected wire at TADPOLE RESERVE from D.24.b.2.5. to D.24.b.9.7.
At 3 p.m. on the 2nd the Company moved from it's quarters to BAPAUME and joined the 167th Infantry Brigade Group for marching out of the area next day.

<u>512th Field Co. R.E</u>: The Company assembled on the FREMICOURT-BAPAUME Road and joined the 168th Infantry Brigade Group for marching out of the area next day.

<u>513th Field Co. R.E</u>: The Company moved from it's billets at DOIGNIES and assembled in LEBUCQUIERE and joined 169th Infantry Brigade Group ready for marching out of the area next day.

<u>3rd December, 1917.</u>

H.Q. R.E. and 3 Field Companies marched out of the area to the ARRAS District.

3. From November 20th to 28th an average of 350 men from Labour Companies were employed on repair and upkeep of the BEUGNY-BOURSIES Road, the pave of which was in an exceedingly bad state. Lieut. Jenkins R.E., and Army Roads Officer attached to the D.E. had charge of this work, on which 8 Foden lorries were continuously employed for bringing up road metal.

4. From Nov. 19 to Nov. 25 each Field Coy had 100 Infantry attached to it for work.

14/12/17.

Lieut.Col.R.E.,
C.R.E., 56th Division.

WAR DIARY
INTELLIGENCE SUMMARY.
(Erase heading not required.)

Army Form C. 2118

WO R₂ 562
101 23

Place	Date	Hour	Summary of Events and Information	Remarks and references to Appendices
	1917			
FREMICOURT	3/12		Moved by train to FOSSEUX	
			Received 56th Divl Warning Order No 737. Had the 56th Divn will move into XIII Corps area on 5th and Commence relief of 3rd Division in the line	
FOSSEUX G3 & Y4	5/12 8/12		Moved to PORTSMOUTH CAMP, G3 & Y4 (Sheet 51B) by road	
	to		Companies were fully engaged on the wiring of the Support and Reserve Lines, over 23,000 yards of double Apron fence being erected	
	18/12		C.R.E. left for leave to United Kingdom.	
	20/12		Major J.D.PARK, 416th (Edinburgh) Field Coy R.E. awarded to act.	

[signature]
& Adjt. R.E.
For C.R.E. 56th Divl Engrs

HQ RE 56 Army Form C. 2118
5th Div Hdq to RE

Vol 24

WAR DIARY
INTELLIGENCE SUMMARY
(Erase heading not required.)

Place	Date	Hour	Summary of Events and Information	Remarks and references to Appendices
G 3 d 7 4 (Sheet 51B)	2/1/16		Issued Order No 124 Copy attached	A
"	4/1		Amendment to Order 124 Copy attached	B
"	5/1		C.R.E. returned from leave. Major ——— returned to Coy	
"	7/1		Issued Order No 125 Copy attached	C
"	8/1		Issued Provisional Order 126 A and 126 B Copies attached	D. E.
"	9/1		Moved by road to Camp at A 20 d 4.3 (Sheet 51 B)	
H 20 d 4.3	10/1		Issued Amendment to Order 125 Copy attached	F
"			Issued Provisional Order 126 C Copy attached	G
"	18/1		Issued Order No 127 Copy attached	H
"	23/1		C.R.E. left for hospital. Capt. Major G.J. Kingsford 513 (London) Field Coy R.E. arrived to act	
"	29/1		C.R.E. returned from hospital Major B.J. Kingsford returned to Coy.	

Capt. & Adjt. R.E.
For C.R.E. 56TH DIVL ENGRS

WAR DIARY

Headquarters,

ROYAL ENGINEERS, 56th Division.

M A R C H

1 9 1 8

Army Form C. 2118

WAR DIARY
or
INTELLIGENCE SUMMARY.
(Erase heading not required.)

Hdqtrs 2nd Aust RE Vol 2

Place	Date 1916	Hour	Summary of Events and Information	Remarks and references to Appendices
G3 A 9 a	1/3 to 24/3		The Field Companies were fully employed in defence work in the Australian area	
	26/3		until	
	29/3		"B" Reserve Brigade was temporarily formed, commander C.R.E. The R.E. Batt. of the Brigade consisted of the 3 Field Companies and 176th Tunnelling Co R.E. & was commanded by Major J.T.F. HENDERSON, 5th Field Co. for Combatant duties.	
	28/29		The Companies were ordered to man JUNCTION REDOUBT, BLANCHE POST and TONGUE POST.	
	30/3		The Division was relieved by the 1st Canadian Division. Headquarters R.E. moved by road to A.C.Q.	

JWOrr
Capt. & Adjt. R.E.
For C.R.E. 50th DIVL ENGRS

56th Divisional Engineers

C. R. E.

56th DIVISION

APRIL 1918.

Army Form C. 2118

WAR DIARY
INTELLIGENCE SUMMARY
(Erase heading not required.)

Hdqtrs 56th Aust R.E.

WO 27

Place	Date 1918	Hour	Summary of Events and Information	Remarks and references to Appendices
ACQ	April 1 to 4		The three Companies were training.	
"	5		Companies were ordered to move to ESTREE CAUCHIE.	
"	8		The Division took over from 1st Canadian Division.	
			Hdqtrs R.E. moved by road to BERNEVILLE.	
BERNEVILLE	23		Divisional front extended by taking over from 15th Division.	
"	8/30		The Divl Engineers were fully employed on trench improvement, dugouts and preparing bridges, RONVILLE and ST SAVEUR Caves for demolition	

John Orr
Capt. & Adjt: R.E.
For C.R.E. 56th DIVL ENGRS.

Army Form C. 2118

WAR DIARY
—or—
INTELLIGENCE SUMMARY.
(Erase heading not required.)

Hdqtrs. 56 Aus R.E.

Place	Date	Hour	Summary of Events and Information	Remarks and references to Appendices
BERNEVILLE	10/5/18		Hdqtrs R.E. moved by road to MARLUS.	
MARLUS	11/31		During the month the field Companies have been fully occupied in defence work of the 5th sector. Trench improvement wiring, dugouts and demolition schemes.	

Arthur Orr
Capt. & Adjt. R.E.
For C.R.E. 56TH DIVL ENGRS

Army Form C. 2118

WAR DIARY
INTELLIGENCE SUMMARY.
(Erase heading not required.)

Hdqrs 56th Div. R.E.

Vol 2

Place	Date	Hour	Summary of Events and Information	Remarks and references to Appendices
WARLUS	1 to 30.6.19		The Field Companies continued work on the defences of the divisional area. Trench improvement, wiring, dugouts and demolition schemes.	

John Orr
Capt. & Adjt. R.E.
For C.R.E. 56th Divl. Engrs.

WAR DIARY or INTELLIGENCE SUMMARY.

Army Form C. 2118

APRIL 56 WB 30

Place	Date	Hour	Summary of Events and Information	Remarks and references to Appendices
WARLUS	1916 July 1st to 14th		The Field Companies continued work on the Divisional area. Trench improvement, wiring, dugouts and demolition schemes	
BEUGIN	15th		Head Qrs R.E. moved by road to BEUGIN 416th Field Coy R.E. entrained to proceed to XVIII Corps School of Inf. Training MARESQUEL	
"	15th to 23rd		512 & 513 Field Companies on intensive training - physical drill, close order drill, open order battle drill, bayonet fighting, Lewis Gun theory and musketry, Musketry	
BAJUS	18th		Head Qrs R.E. moved to BAJUS.	
"	23rd to 31st		The three Field Companies employed on intensive training	
"	23rd		416th Field Coy R.E. rejoined 56th Division & commenced training	

Meersch
Lt. Col. R.E.
C.R.E. 56th Divl. Engrs.

HQ RE 56D
Vol 31

WAR DIARY
or
INTELLIGENCE SUMMARY.

Army Form C. 2118

Place	Date	Hour	Summary of Events and Information	Remarks and references to Appendices
BAJUS	August 1918 1st		56th Division takes over a sector of the line from 1st Canadian Division	
			The Head Quarters RE moved by road to WARLUS. Field Companies employed on Dugouts & Demolition upkeep.	
WARLUS	18th		Head Quarters RE moved by road to LE CAUROY. Field Cos training with a view to impending offensive operations.	
LE CAUROY	22nd		Head Quarters RE moved by road to BAVINCOURT en route for sector of attack 23rd	
BAVINCOURT	24th		Head Quarters RE moved by road to BLAIREVILLE QUARRY to Advanced Divisional Head Quarters to join CRE and Div HQ	
BLAIREVILLE QUARRY	27th		Head Quarters RE moved forward by road to BOISLEUX ST MARC (S14 S.W.) Field Companies employed on reconnoitering for water & on water supply, Tunnels & Caves, Bridges, Roads & Tracks.	

Signed
Lt. Col. R.E.
C.R.E. 56th DIV. ENGRS.

Vol 32

War Diaries
September 1918

56th Divisional Engineers

Headquarters
512th (London) Field Coy RE
513th   "   "   "   "
416th (Edinboro') "   "   "
56th Divl Signal Coy. R.E.

Army Form C. 2118

WAR DIARY
or
INTELLIGENCE SUMMARY.
(Erase heading not required.)

Instructions regarding War Diaries and Intelligence Summaries are contained in F.S. Regs., Part II. and the Staff Manual respectively. Title pages will be prepared in manuscript.

Place	Date	Hour	Summary of Events and Information	Remarks and references to Appendices
BOISLEUX ST. MARC.	Septr.1st.		Field Companies on water supply, searching for booby traps, minor bridge work and erection of baths for troops subsequent to operations. 2/Lieut. McGill R.E. assumed duties of Acting/Adjt. R.E. from 18th August, while Capt. Orr R.E. the Adjutant was in hospital.	
LES FOSSES FARM.	"	9th.	Div. H.Q. and H.Q. R.E. to LES FOSSES FARM, transferring to XXIInd Corps. 512th & 513th Field Companies in the line, principally employed on accommodation for our Infantry in area recently captured from enemy. 416th Field Coy. in reserve principally employed on water supply and baths. During this period 513th Field Coy. carried out some very important but difficult and dangerous reconnaissances in "No Man's" land over the area flooded by the SENSEE& it was important to ascertain what the possibilities of advance over this flood by either ourselves or the enemy were and whether the flood was rising or falling. As a result of these reconnaissances 2/Lieut. E.J.Giles R.E., 513th (London) Fd.Co.R.E. was awarded a Military Cross.	
ILLERS LES AGNI- COURT.	"	26th.	H.Q. R.E. moved to advanced Div.H.Q. at VILLERS LES CAGNICOURT for operations beginning next day for which the whole of the R.E. had been preparing for 7 days.	
	"	27th	Operation of crossing the CANAL DU NORD North and South of the ARRAS-CAMBRAI Road began. Canadian Corps attacked at 5-20 a.m., crossing a mile South of the main road and moving Northward along the East bank of the CANAL without mopping up. 11th Division crossed after them and proceeded Northward at a distance of half a mile from the CANAL DU NORD, capturing OISY LE VERGER in the evening. The 169th Inf. Bde. of the 56th Divn. were timed to cross the CANAL North & South of MARQUION between 10 and 12 in the morning. The Divisional Engineers had the duty of preparing crossing for this Infantry Brigade over the CANAL DU NORD and the AGACHE STREAM so far as these were obstacles, which they proved to be. On the South of the road 512th Field Coy. pushed back the enemy, siezed siezed the crossing and made the necessary bridges for both CANAL DU NORD and AGACHE STREAM by 1-30 p.m. On the North of the road, after a well executed reconnaissance by 513th Field Coy. Officers it was found that the CANAL proved no obstacle but 416th Field Coy. successfully and in time bridged the AGACHE and a small tributary. In the evening the attack had progressed so far Northward that it was possible to throw	

throw/

Army Form C. 2118.

WAR DIARY
or
INTELLIGENCE SUMMARY.
(Erase heading not required.)

sheet 2.

Place	Date	Hour	Summary of Events and Information	Remarks and references to Appendices
			throw/a	
	Septr. 28th		a pontoon bridge across the CANAL just South of SAUCHY CAUCHY. This was done by 513th Field Coy. by 5 a.m. with the assistance of the 1/5th Cheshire(Pioneers) Regt. who had heavy ramping to do. Engineer reconnaissances of water supply, bridges, roads, booby traps, land mines, enemy Engineer stores, etc, carried out by Divnl. Engineers and 1/5th Cheshire Pioneer Battalion. Road repair made. Another pontoon bridge thrown across the river opposite SAUCHY CAUCHY by 512th Field Coy. R.E. 416th Field Coy. were ordered to take soundings for a heavy track bridge to replace pontoon bridge South of SAUCHY CAUCHY.	
	" 29th.		416th Field Coy. building heavy bridge. 512th Field Coy. reconnoitred for heavy bridge over AGACHE in SAUCHY CAUCHY and mended existing bridge. 416th Field Coy. assisting the forward infantry.	
	" 30th.		The 416th Field Coy. completed heavy bridge 90' span, 18' high on steel cubes (2 main piers, 2 shore(grip piers) to carry all traffic except tanks, in 6' of water, in 25 hours, which was stated to be the best time he had known by O.C. 1st Army, Advanced Heavy Bridging Depot, who supplied the stores. 512th Field Coy. completed their heavy bridge and approaches to it. 513th Field Coy. took over maintenance of all wagon and foot bridges over the CANAL and began back area work. H.Q. R.E. is still at VILLERS LES CAGNICOURT. The list of congratulations received by the Divisional Engineers and Pioneer Battalion on the occasion of the bridging during these operations is attached.	
	7/10/18.			

Lieut.Col.R.E.,
C.R.E.,56th Division.

-1-

C.E. XXIInd. Corps
No. E.B. 724.

To:- G. O. C.
56th. Division.

C.R.E.
56th DIVISION.
No. E34/4.
Date.........

War Diary

The Corps Commander directs me to convey his congratulations on the good work done by the technical troops of your Division, especially in connection with the bridging of the CANAL DU NORD, for the very successful operation carried out by your Division yesterday.

I am to add that General GODLEY would be glad if you would express his thanks to all ranks of the Royal Engineers and Pioneer Battalion and his appreciation of their good work which he is convinced largely contributed to the success of the attack.

(Sd) A.E. Panet, Brig-Genl.
Chief Engineer, XXIInd. Corps.

Sept. 28th. 1918.

****

-2-

C. R. E.

I am very glad to forward this and wish to add my own thanks for the good work done.

C. Hull, Major Genl.
Commanding 56th. Division.

28-9-18.

O.C. 512th (London) Fd.Co.R.E.
O.C. 513th (London) Fd.Co.R.E.
O.C. 516th (Edinbr) Fd.Co.R.E.
O.C. 1/5th Cheshire Pioneers.
- - - - -

      I have pleasure in forwarding herewith a copy of the First Army Commander's congratulations on recent work done by R.E. and Pioneers and shall be glad if you will bring same to the notice of the troops.

Lieut.Col.R.E.
C.R.E., 56th Divn.

5/10/18.

STOCK REPORT – showing material on hand at :-

Article	Carpenter shop Dump. ARRAS – G.22.d.22.	Forward Dump NORTH ALLEY M.6.c.10.90.	"C" Company Dump G.35.d.7.5.
re, barbed, coils	590	350	300
" plain	–	–	–
kes, screw, long	60	180	100
" " medium	320	–	100
" " short	–	400	–
ndbags.	9260	–	–
e sets, standard	+	215	80
gging 3' pieces	10	260	20
" 4' "	–	300	40
" beams & rails	–	45	8
" beam shoes	–	65	10
Props	45	50	25
" (split)	15	–	–

4th Divn.

First Army No. M.14 (G).
4th Divn. No. G.A. 109.
Corps No. G.10/79.

The Army Commander has read with great interest the report on the bridging operation over the Canal du Nord carried out by the Canadian Engineers and the Field Companies, R.E. of the 11th and 12th Corps during the recent operations.

He wishes to express his admiration of the special efforts made by the Engineers and their Commanders, and to congratulate all concerned on their steadiness under fire and the success which attended their labours.

The successful execution of a difficult manoeuvre in the face of the enemy was greatly assisted by the admirable work of the Royal and Canadian Engineers.

First Army.
3rd October,1918.

sd/ A.S.Gordon, Major-Genrl.
General Staff, First Army.

Gen.S.

The G.O.C. has great pleasure in forwarding the attached First Army Letter.

sd/ E.G.S.McKean, Major for
Lieut-Colonel,
General Staff.

4th October,1918.

 " " " "

 " " " "

 " " " "

Operator the same.

Operator the same.

G.H.Q. 2/10/18.

Dear Mozley,

I have just read an account of your bridging operations. Please let me congratulate you and all concerned, it was a very fine performance and makes us all proud of the R.E.
The Commander-in-Chief is full of praise for the Engineers and he has reason to be.

Yours sincerely,

G.M.HEATH.

- - - - - - - -
- S -

O.C. 512th (London) Fd.Co.R.E.
O.C. 513th (London) Fd.Co.R.E.
O.C. 416th (Edinbr) Fd.Co.R.E.
O.C. 1/5th Cheshire Pioneers.
- - - - - - - - - -

The C.R.E. has much pleasure in circulating to the Field Companies and Pioneer Battn. the above copy of a letter which he has received from the Engineer-in-Chief today.
Would you please bring this to the notice of the troops.

sd/ E.N.MOZLEY,
Lieut.Col.R.E.,
C.R.E., 56th Division.

3/10/18.

done. GRANT has been CQMS for 12 months in England, and for 9 months in France before being promoted to C.S.M.

WHITELOCK has been CQMS at ESHER for nearly two years in England and would be all the better for experience in France.

H G Medge
Major RE
OC 512 London Field Coy

23-6-17

R., XXIInd Corps.

I forward following account of yesterday's operations by 25th Divnl. Engineers and 1/5th Battalion Cheshire Regt. (Pioneers):-

1. The 169th Inf. Bde. hoped to cross the canal and the AMACHE at W.15.a.9.7. at 10 a.m. and at W.9.b.3.3 a 11 a.m. Strong hostile resistance especially by M.Gs. prevented Infantry reaching woodlands West of CANAL. Nevertheless Lieut. Midman, 415th Field Co.R.E. and Sergt. Treble R.E. worked their way through W.9.c and across ground swept by M.G.fire in W.9.a to the woods in W.9.a & b and to the CANAL itself and saw the enemy on the opposite bank running Northwards. They reached the canal at 11-30a. one hour and twenty mins. before any Infantry entered these woods. In the same way, Lieut. Robertson, 412th Field Co.R.E., with his section fought his way to the canal at W.15.a.9.7 by 12-45 p.m., met the enemy, extended his sappers, drove the enemy back and took possession of the canal crossing at 12-45 p.m. at which hour he reported to his O.C. that he was short of S.A.A. but as Infantry were now approaching 400 yds. behind he thought he could hold on. Lieut. Midman had two out of his three runners wounded during his reconnaissance and Lieut. Robertson had two men wounded. The Company of the Cheshire Regiment with Lieut. Robertson did admirable combatant work and took 12 prisoners.

2. Time Table of crossings effected was as follows:-
(a) South of Canal, Cork raft footbridge and plank footbridge thrown across water and marsh about W.15.a.9.7 by 12-30 p.m.
Infantry footbridges thrown across AMACHE in W.15.b at 1-45 p.m.
Both of the above by 212th Field Co.R.E. who subsequently reconnoitred WANCOURT FARM W.10.c.3.4 and was then sent into reserve.
(b) The Canal at W.9.b.3.3 was no obstacle but the AMACHE at W.10.a.5.7 and streams running between the CANAL and the AMACHE were bridged for Inf. by 415th Field Co. and 415th Field Co. at 3-4 p.m. Subsequently these bridges and the marshy tracks between them were made fit for horsed wheeled transport by the morning of the 29th.

3. By 6 p.m. Infantry advanced Northwards on both sides of the CANAL and enabled reconnaissance to be made of the best place for throwing a crossing for guns proceeding along the W.2 - Q.34 road. An officer of 415th Field Co. selected a good site and sent back for timber for trestling. At 10.p.m. however, the C.R.E. determined that the drop from the bank to water at this site was not too great for a pontoon bridge and the pontoons were ordered up. The message to them was delayed, but at 12-30 a.m. 29th they passed point W.1.d.3.2 on the main road and thence proceeded at a fast trot to the site of the bridge Q.34.d.35.30 with the result that the 415th Field Co. had the bridge completed by 5 a.m. and the Company of the Cheshire Battn. working with them got through the heavy work of cutting down the ramps by the same hour. This bridge carries guns and the approaches to metalled roads on both banks are reasonably good.

4. In addition to the above a great deal of repair to roads on the West bank after considerable shell fire was executed by the 1/5th Battn. Cheshire Regt. whose work left nothing to be desired.

sd/ E.N.MOZLEY
Lieut.Col.R.E.,
C.R.E., 25th Division.

28/8/18.

5. At 10 p.m. 27th, the XXIInd Corps ordered a broken culvert on the lorry road at P.20.b.90.45 to be repaired. The 415th Fd.Coy.R.E. turned out and completed it by 5-30 a.m.

WAR DIARY
or
INTELLIGENCE SUMMARY.
(Erase heading not required.)

Army Form C. 2118

Place	Date	Hour	Summary of Events and Information	Remarks and references to Appendices
VILLERS LES CAGNICOURT.	Oct. 1st to 14th.		Head Qrs R.E. at VILLERS CAGNICOURT. Field Companies employed on bridging and maintenance of Bridges over CANAL DU NORD and CANAL DE LA SENSEE & RIVER AGACHE; also damming & clearing CANAL DE LA SENSEE to protect surrounding country from flooding; also carrying out important reconnaissances for sites of bridges, water levels, water supply, roads etc.	A
	15th.		Head Qrs R.E. moved by road to MAROEUIL.(into Army reserve) Field Companies training - physical drill, close & open order drill, route marches - and giving instructions to Infantry in use of Berthon Boats at ARRAS & LOUEZ.	A

Lt. Col. R.E.
C.R.E. 56th Division.

C.R.E. 56th Division.

Account of operations carried out by ROYAL ENGINEERS of the 56th Division, and Pioneers - Nov. 2nd to 11th 1918.

Novr. 2nd. 56th Div. R.E. took over from 49th D.E. The principal work was placing the broken bridge over the river RHONELLE, East of FAMARS (K.10.c.1.7., Sheet 51A N.E.) This bridge was placed over the original alignment and was of a span of 58 feet.

It was built in three days on two intermediate piers of steel cubes. The Bridge was handed over at mid-day Nov. 4th when the piers and abutments were erected but the roadway had not been placed, to 4th D.E. 512th Fd. Co. was in charge of this bridge.

416th Fd.Co. had charge of the maintenance of Weldon Trestle Bridges at each side of the bridge K.10.c.1.7., and was also engaged with Pioneer assistance in clearing the roadway at K.20.d.91 where the VALENCIENNES - LE QUESNOY railway crosses it. The roadway had been entirely blocked at K.13.b.X.3.

513th Field Co. was also engaged in clearing the road at K.13.b.73. where the railway had been dropped upon it.

1/5th Cheshire Regt. (56th Div. Pioneer Batt) was employed on roadwork immediately West and East of FAMARS.

4th. Three Field Cos and Pioneer Batt. moved to SAULTAIN with the advancing Division, the enemy being in retreat. On arrival, 416th Fd. Co. was held in readiness for pontooning over the river AUNNELLE with the whole of the D.E. bridging equipment. The other Field Cos and Pioneer Batt. were engaged on making Horse Traffic deviations around the numerous craters in the vicinity of SAULTAIN.

5th. 416th and 512th Field Cos moved to SEBOURQUIAUX. 513th Fd. Co. moved to SEBOURG. At this period, 416th Fd. Co. had attached to it one Company of Pioneers and the other two Field Cos each had attached two platoons of Pioneers.

416th Fd. Co. erected a 5-bay Weldon Trestle Bridge over the AUNNELLE at A.14.c.9.7. (Sheet 51) where the main bridge through the village had been broken.

512th Fd. Co. were given the task of mxing making a bridge for all traffic except tanks at the same site. This bridge was made in three spans (total 62 feet) The two intermediate piers being on single tier cubes. It was completed on November 7th. Pioneer Battalion was employed on making good roads and craters between SAULTAIN and RIVER AUNELLE.

7th. 416th Field Company moved to ANGREAU with the D.E. Bridging equipment. The xxixx whole Company, with two platoons of Pioneers was employed on making good a ford and its approaches across the GRAND HONELLE at B.12.c.4.1. which two brigades of Artillery had to cross to get into action early next morning.

512th and 513th Fd. Cos. also moved to ANGREAU.

8th. 513th Fd. Co. with the Pioneer Batt. was given the task of clearing the obstruction on the road at B.20.c.3.1. where a 50 ft high railway viaduct had been dropped on the road by the enemy, leaving a mound 40 yards along the length of road and 20 ft. high. This was cleared by evening.

416th Fd. Co. was in charge of all other crossings within the Divisional area across the GRAND HONELLE (Fords only)

9th The Division moved to FAYT LE FRANC.

512th Field Co. placed a three span Weldon Trestle Bridge at B.20.c.1.0. close to where the main road bridge over the GRAND HONNELLE had been broken down. All three Field Cos and Pioneer Batt. moved to AUTREPPE. The Pioneer Batt. was employed on road work East of the GRAND HONNELLE including two large craters in AUTREPPE. 416th Fd. Co. made good for Horse Traffic the broken bridge at B.17.a.8.8.

513th Fd. Co. made temporary Weldon Trestle Bridge over the GRAND HONNELLE and took it up, at about B.20.c.1.0.

2

Nov. 10th.
513th Field Co. moved to FAYT LE FRANC, 416th Field Co. moved to DESSOUS (D.9) and 512th Field Co. moved to D.7. Pioneer Batt. moved to ATHIS and were employed on roads East of the GRAND HONELLE.

416th Fd. Co. made good for horse traffic, and subsequently for all loads except tanks, the broken bridges at D.8.a.Central and D.8.d.9.6.

512th Fd. Co. Made good for Horse transport and subsequently for all loads except tanks, bridges at C.24.b.1.6., D.13.a.2.6., and D.7.b.7.9. The above bridges were all of from 7 to 12 ft. span.

Throughout the above operations the following reconnaissances were made daily:-
(a) Water Supply in villages by a party of 416th Fd. Co.
(b) Forward Bridges by a party of 512th Fd.Co.
(c) Enemy dumps and civilian engineering material by a party of 513th Fd. Company.
(d) Roads and enemy tramways by a party of 1/5 Bn. Ches. Regt.

15/11/18.

Sd/E. MOZLEY, Lt. Colonel, R.E.
C.R.E., 56th Division.

Army Form C. 2118

WAR DIARY
or
INTELLIGENCE SUMMARY.
(Erase heading not required.)

Instructions regarding War Diaries and Intelligence Summaries are contained in F.S. Regs., Part II. and the Staff Manual respectively. Title pages will be prepared in manuscript.

Place	Date	Hour	Summary of Events and Information	Remarks and references to Appendices
	1 Nov.		H.Q.R.E. move to BOUCHAIN, via road.	
	3 "		Move to MONCHAUX.	
	5 "		Move to SAULTAIN, by road.	
	9 "		Move to FAYT LE FRANC.	
	11 "		Armistice signed, 11 a.m. Up to this date Field Cos. were chiefly employed in maintaining forward communication, repairing and erecting bridges etc.	
	19 "		Lt. Col. Mozley, R.E. left for U.K. on 30 days leave. Major Steers R.E. assumes duties.	
	22 "		2/Lt. J.V.T. Henwood a/Adjt, left for U.K. on ordinary leave. Lieut. McGill R.E. assumes duties.	
	28 "		Move to HARVENGT.	
			After the Armistice day work was carried on chiefly clearing and cleaning roads. When time and conditions permitted the employment of Companies was diverted more to training and improving sanitary conditions of the various Communes which they occupied, whilst recreational programmes were carried out in spare time. Educational scheme put into motion towards the end of the month.	

Lt MAOITE
for CRE cf Division

Army Form C. 2118

WA Re 56 D 10/2/4

WAR DIARY
or
INTELLIGENCE SUMMARY.
(Erase heading not required.)

Instructions regarding War Diaries and Intelligence Summaries are contained in F.S. Regs., Part II. and the Staff Manual respectively. Title pages will be prepared in manuscript.

Place	Date	Hour	Summary of Events and Information	Remarks and references to Appendices
HARVENGT.	1918 Decr. 1st.-31st.		The three Field Companies engaged on erection of baths, messes, erection and maintenance of bridges (where required by Division) and general improvements in accommodation.	
			A good proportion of the R.E. entered into the various educational classes arranged, and, keen interest has been aroused by the large sports programme that has been put into operation.	
			Demobilisation starts, but during the month only about a dozen pivotal men have been despatched for demobilisation.	

Ellworthy
Lt/Col. R.E.
C.R.E. 56th. Division.

2353 Wt.W2344/1454 700,000 5/15 D,D,&L. A.D.S.S./Forms/C. 2118.

Original

56th Divnl. Engineers

War Diary

January 1919.

Army Form C. 2118

WAR DIARY
or
INTELLIGENCE SUMMARY.

(Erase heading not required.)

Instructions regarding War Diaries and Intelligence Summaries are contained in F. S. Regs., Part II. and the Staff Manual respectively. Title pages will be prepared in manuscript.

Place	Date	Hour	Summary of Events and Information	Remarks and references to Appendices
HARVENGT	January 1st. 1919		H.Q.R.E. remained at HARVENGT during the whole of the month. 3 O.R. from H.Q.R.E. were demobilised and 240 O.R. demobilised from the three Field Companies during the month.	

Lt. Col. R.E.
C.R.E. 56th. Division.

Original

War Diary

February 1919

56th Divnl. Engineers

Army Form C. 2118.

WAR DIARY
or
INTELLIGENCE SUMMARY.
(Erase heading not required.)

Place	Date	Hour	Summary of Events and Information	Remarks and references to Appendices
HARVENGT.	1919. Feby. 1st to 28th.		H.Q.R.E. remained at HARVENGT, during the whole of the month. Four O.R. from H.Q.R.E. and 5 Officers and 118 O.R. demobilized from the three Field Companies during the month.	

Captain & Adjt.R.E.
for C.R.E. 56th Division.

Army Form C. 2118.

WAR DIARY
or
INTELLIGENCE SUMMARY.
(Erase heading not required.)

R.E. HQ.

Place	Date	Hour	Summary of Events and Information	Remarks and references to Appendices
HARVENGT.	1919. March. 1st to 29th.		Demobilizing proceeding - Field Companies practically down to Cadre "B" strength.	
QUAREGNON.	29th.		H.Q.R.E. moved by road to QUAREGNON.	

for C.R.E. 56th Division.
Captain & Adjt. R.E.

Army Form C. 2118.

WAR DIARY
or
INTELLIGENCE SUMMARY.

(Erase heading not required.)

C.R.E. 56th DIVISION.

Instructions regarding War Diaries and Intelligence Summaries are contained in F.S. Regs., Part II. and the Staff Manual respectively. Title pages will be prepared in manuscript.

Place	Date	Hour	Summary of Events and Information	Remarks and references to Appendices
QUAREGNON	1919. April 1st to 30th.		H.Q. 56th Div. R.E. remained at Quaregnon during th whole of the month.	
	7th.		Capt & Adjt. J.V.T. Henwood to C.R.E. Mons Sub Area.	
	8th.		Capt. J. Robertson, 512th (London) Field Co. R.E. took over from Capt. Henwood as A/Adjt.	

N. Carter
Lieut. & A/Adjt.RE.
for C.R.E. 56th Division.

Army Form C. 2118.

HQ RE 56D
51 50 ceased

WAR DIARY
or
INTELLIGENCE SUMMARY.
(Erase heading not required.)

Instructions regarding War Diaries and Intelligence Summaries are contained in F. S. Regs., Part II. and the Staff Manual respectively. Title pages will be prepared in manuscript.

Place	Date	Hour	Summary of Events and Information	Remarks and references to Appendices
	1919			
QUAREGNON	May 16.17		H.Q. RE 56th Divn remained at QUAREGNON.	
"		18-	Cadre of H.Q. RE entrained for U.K. at JEMAPPES Station	

Signature
Capt. & Adjt. R.E.
For C.R.E. 56TH DIVL ENGS